SUNDAY
IN TUDOR AND STUART TIMES

SUNDAY
IN
TUDOR AND STUART TIMES

BY

W. B. WHITAKER, M.A.
(BRISTOL)

LONDON
THE HOUGHTON PUBLISHING CO.
REGENT HOUSE, REGENT STREET, W.1

To

MY WIFE

without whose encouragement this book
could not have been written.

First published - - - 1933

PREFACE

SOME years ago I was asked to explain how we obtained our distinctive English Sunday. Realizing my inability to give an adequate reply I sought for some book which would supply the information. There appeared to be none and fairly exhaustive research since has failed to discover one. In view of the controversy aroused to-day by the question of Sunday observance it is strange that the only modern treatment of the early history of the English Sunday is contained in an essay recently published by Mr. W. P. Baker in a book entitled *Englishmen at Rest and Play* and this only came to my notice after I had completed the writing of my book. As no detailed study of the way in which Sunday was kept in the sixteenth and seventeenth centuries ever seems to have been made the primary object of this book is to attempt to fill a gap that at present exists in our literature.

The question of Sunday observance was a keenly debated one in Tudor and Stuart days and a multitude of books appeared on the matter then. Not all of those are mentioned in the Bibliography attached to this study because many of them are of no use whatever in throwing light upon the way people acted on the Sunday of that time.

For several years I have used Dr. Williams's Library in London and I welcome this opportunity to thank the Librarian and his assistants for their unfailing courtesy and help.

Finally I desire to acknowledge my great debt of gratitude to Emeritus Professor G. H. Leonard, M.A., of Bristol University. While he is in no way responsible for this book or any of its faults of omission or commission yet anything that is of value in it is due to the inspiration and training which I received from him and from those associated with him when I was a student at Bristol.

W. B. WHITAKER.

Gravesend,
   September, 1932.

FOREWORD

by

Professor G. H. Leonard, M.A. (Cambridge) Emeritus Professor of Modern History in the University of Bristol.

THIS little book on the English Sunday is opportune. Once again in the History of our country the "Sunday question" is one which is agitating many minds. If there should be any "Observance" of the first day of the week, in what way should it stand apart from other days? Should it be a day of rest—the Jewish Sabbath, necessarily modified somewhat to the conditions of our time, or should it be a public "holiday" on which work—though inevitable for many who minister to the needs of holiday-makers—for the generality of men should be reduced to a minimum? At the moment of writing the particular issue uppermost in men's minds seems to be the controversy which centres round the Sunday School and the Cinema. There are those who hold—if indeed there must be a choice—that it is better for children in their most impressionable years to be taught the rudiments of religion in the old-fashioned—or is it possible to conceive of a *new*-fashioned—Sunday School?—or succumb to the allurements of the film.

On the particular question of the time, and on the general question of the "observance" of Sunday, people take sides. Controversy is rife. Many who are sincerely anxious to take a reasonable view do not know what to think, they are not clear about the principles involved, not fully persuaded in their own minds. "One man esteemeth one day above another: another esteemeth every day alike." If there was confusion in the early church what are we to think in *this* day of grace? If the searching of scriptures is not our habit, and the divided opinions of the Fathers, primitive or puritan, are indifferent to us, can we

find any verdicts of History, ancient or modern, to guide
us in our decisions?

To many of us this book will be not only of interest but
I think of some real use. The writer no doubt has opinions
of his own, but he is not writing as a propagandist. He is a
careful student, anxious to get at the real facts and the
genuine opinions of the men who were making history in
this country at a certain definite period. Here he has given
us the benefit of his researches. Some of the results perhaps
came to him as something of a surprise as they may well
come to many of his readers. Most of us talk glibly of the
"English Sunday" and of the "Puritans" without any
very clear knowledge of what these terms mean. We talk
of the "Continental Sunday", without having made any
very careful examination of the *Catholic* point of view
concerning its "observance". We do not, as a matter of
fact, know our History. We do not recognize the vein of
Sabbatarianism in the Mediaeval Church. We are not
aware that English Puritanism is not all of a piece, nor
how, or *when*—this English Sunday of ours evolved. In
this little book Mr. Whitaker is concerned to tell the most
important part of this story. He begins with the beginning
of the Reformation and ends with the legislation of 1677,
when under Charles II, of all people, it was made definitely
clear that all unnecessary Sunday labour and trading
must come to an end, and the Sabbatarian programme
seemed fairly complete. It is a period of many changes,
but what becomes clear as years passed by is that, in spite
of action and reaction in high places, a tradition was growing up that Sunday should be recognized as a day apart.
Earlier legislation had put a stop to the familiar Sunday
sports, and now, in 1677, the customary labour of the week-
day was definitely and finally disallowed.

It appears to be a mistake to suppose that a stricter
observance of "the Lord's Day" was contemporaneous
with the Reformation. The earliest of the new teachers
were divided in their opinions as the Lollards had been at
an earlier time, some holding that men must devote themselves on that day wholly to "ghostly works behovable
for man's soul", others, remembering that man was not
"made for the Sabbath", believing that honest work at all

events, was compatible with prayer and worship on the same day. In the well known hymn of William Kethe, it should be remembered also, that men were called upon to serve God "with mirth"—the too familiar emendation which encourages us to serve him "with fear" belongs to a later and grimmer period—a period too when the grave word "fear" had acquired a different and a grimmer meaning.

In these pages we are shown how the pendulum swayed to and fro, *e.g.*, James I's Proclamation of the *Book of Sports* in 1606 to be commended by every parson in his Parish Church, and the Ordinance of the Long Parliament in 1664, forbidding "Wrastlings, Ringing of Bells for Pleasure . . . Games, Sports or Pastimes whatever" on the Sabbath Day.

How far the various laws and ordinances were regularly enforced in different parts of the country it is impossible to say, but, through all, certain broad principles were gradually emerging—with a new and steady respect for Sunday—for days set apart—not only as the pillars

"On which heav'n's palace archèd lies,"

but also on which man's true well-being here below depends. Not only the Puritan but the Anglican now becomes more careful for the closer "observance" of the day as one consecrated for the higher interests of man. When the Commonwealth came to an end the pendulum swung once more but "the persons restored" did not, as a matter of fact, go "just antipodes to the interval time," and the "Society for the Reformation of Manners" of 1690, though beyond the period of our consideration here, was at least in view. With Queen Anne, the last of the Stuarts, England was clearly settling down to the normal Sunday—the *English* Sunday—as we know it in comparatively recent History— the day which we are given to understand by a caustic observer might seem "as gloomy to foreigners as our English climate, but for most Englishmen," he adds, "is a manifest proof of English superiority in virtue."

It may be that we Englishmen are a little too "confident of Heaven's applause", that we have been too consciously endeavouring to make our "moral being our prime care", and yet to have something of the true "fear" of God in our hearts, to try to "fix on good alone", to rest on a "right foundation" in quality and act—if some such ideals—not wholly beyond our grasp—as those Wordsworth had in mind when he wrote that very English poem *The Happy Warrior*, are in the general estimation connected with the English character, and if, in these days, the reputation of doing justly and loving mercy—if not always walking quite humbly with our God—is, as may well be the case, closely connected with the "English Sunday" with its teaching and hallowed associations, and if there is any real danger that some of the advantages such a day has brought us are in our day seriously endangered, can we hope, looking around us at this critical time, that the prospect is anything but a grave one, not only for our country, but for the great world causes for which I believe we Englishmen—with all our patent faults—still stand.

It may be taken for granted that all are agreed that, in some way or other, one day of the week should be "kept" —some day—not a day to be thought of as one for which man was made—but like the Sabbath as conceived in the Gospel, made for man himself, his interests, and his well being—not, surely, excluding the highest spiritual interests of which he is capable. In our own country changes in the manner of its keeping have been many. From a close study of the past, from experiments old and new, from failure and success—given a clear understanding of the deep issues involved, wisdom, tolerance, and good English common sense—surely we should be able to learn many things to guide us, in these difficult times, how best to arrange an "observance" of Sunday in the national interest, suited to the genius of our people and the new age in which we live.

Clifton, Bristol.
November, 1932.

CONTENTS

SUNDAY
IN TUDOR AND STUART TIMES

CHAPTER I

INTRODUCTION AND REIGN OF HENRY VIII

It has long been a common assumption that the beliefs,
customs and practices of the English Sunday, as distinct from what is usually termed the Continental
Sunday, originated in the times of the Puritans. Such
a postulate is, however, at best only a half-truth.
What is meant in that connection by the word Puritan?
The utterer of the statement and the hearer may
interpret it quite differently. Probably neither stops
to consider what he really means by it. It is one of
those glib terms that slip so easily from the tongue or
the pen of even the historian. The word Puritan
covered at different times, and at the same time,
people with very different ideas and ideals. There
were Puritans within the State Church and also Dissenting Puritans. There were Puritans so called because
they wished to purify the ceremonies of religion and
Puritans who wished to purify the morals of the community. To which class of Puritans must the origin of
the English Sunday be ascribed?

Another question, the answer to which is involved in
the consideration of the use of the term Puritan is:
"*When* did the English Sunday begin?" If it be
possible to determine that with any degree of certainty
there will be closely connected with it the query: "*Why*
did it begin when it did?" Given the answer to these
questions there should be an inquiry into the effect

upon the lives of the people of the establishment of this new practice or observance. The social aspect of the English Sunday seems to have been strangely neglected even by social historians.

Unless the historian attempt a world-wide and age-long survey he must necessarily fix certain boundaries to his investigation. Such boundaries, like those of many countries, will be a mixture of the natural and the artificial. It will be so in the present case. The beginning of the Reformation in England seems to denote a sufficiently natural boundary on the one hand, while the Act of 1677 will be the much more artificial dividing line upon the other.

The aridity of the general religious life of England in the first thirty years of the sixteenth century needs no further proof at this time than has been adduced by countless writers on the subject of the Reformation. The stream of purity and freshness of men like Colet, one of St. Paul's great deans, and of Sir Thomas More could not irrigate such a waste. At such a time we should not expect to find any particular significance given to the observance of Sunday. When almost all religious customs and ceremonies had become mere dry bones, the Sunday could hardly be expected to escape. When the dry bones became re-vitalized and re-shaped the Sunday would share the transformation.

Attendance at Divine Worship once or twice upon the Sunday had, of course, been the usual, as it was the compulsory, thing right through the Middle Ages. But that very formal observance left a great part of the day unprovided for. Generally speaking, people had exercised a great deal of freedom in the choice of ways and means for passing the time on that day. Most of the people considered that the greater part of the day could be devoted to recreation and jollification. Various attempts had been made by the State to regulate to a certain extent what was done on the Sunday. For example, in the reign of Richard II a statute for-

bade the playing of tennis, football and similar games
on the Sunday, so that the people might devote the
time to archery.[1] In the reign of Henry VI it was
found necessary to pass a law prohibiting the holding
of fairs and markets upon the Sunday.[2] Yet such
regulations certainly did not entirely succeed, and for
the average pre-Reformation Englishman the Sunday
was a day upon which, having made a formal appearance at his Parish Church, he was free to spend his time
in the tavern or on the village green, with the added
excitement of a fair or wake or church-ale on some
special Sunday. Affairs of local and national importance, too, were often transacted upon the Sunday. To
take but one example, the accounts of the Corporation
of Lydd, Kent, during the fifteenth century show that
most of the business transactions of the Corporation
took place on the Sunday.[3]

The English Reformation being at first political
rather than religious, and Henry VIII being himself
loath to make changes in religious customs and usages,
we might expect that little or nothing would be said or
done about the observance of Sunday in Henry's reign.
It is therefore somewhat surprising and significant that
the way the people spent the Sunday did engage the
attention of the authorities quite early in the years
following the break away from Rome. As early as 1536
Feasts of Dedication in connection with Churches were
restricted to the first Sunday in October on the grounds
that they occasioned idleness and riot.[4] In 1539 Convocation brought out a book of ceremonies which
stated that: "The Sundays are to be continued and
employed in the service of God, to hear the word
preached, to give thanks for the benefits which we
receive daily. And that day is much to be regarded,
both for the antiquity, and also for that it is a memorial

[1] Statute 12, Richard II.
[2] Statute 27, Henry VI.
[3] *Historical Manuscripts Commission:* Fifth Report (1876) p. 517.
[4] Injunctions of Henry VIII, 1536. (See Prynne, *Canterburies Doome*, p. 130.)

of Christ's resurrection: whereby we ought to be
stirred to rest our minds from earthly things to heavenly
contemplations of Christ's glorified nature."[1] This statement makes no direct reference to the admissibility or
otherwise of Sunday games, but it is of interest as
showing the grounds upon which the Anglican Church
was basing its claims for the observance of Sunday.
The most important document, however, in this connection, as it is also the lengthiest, is the statement
about the Fourth Commandment contained in *A
Necessary Doctrine and Erudition of any Christian
Man* published in 1543 by authority and sometimes
known as *The King's Book*.

This statement of 1543 begins by pointing out that
the Hebrew word which gives us the English word
'sabbath' means 'rest' but that "this precept of the
Sabbath, as concerning rest from bodily labour the
seventh day, is ceremonial, and pertaineth only unto
the Jews in the Old Testament, before the coming of
Christ, and pertaineth not unto us Christian people in
the New Testament. Nevertheless, as concerning the
spiritual rest which is figured and signified by this
corporal rest, that is to say, rest from the carnal works
of the flesh, and all manner of sin, this precept is moral
and remaineth still". This shows the Church at this
date repudiating entirely the position, which was to
be so keenly debated in a century or less, that the
Fourth Commandment was literally binding on the
Christian. The statement continues to say: "we be
bound by this precept at certain times to cease from
bodily labour and to give our minds entirely and wholly
unto God, to hear the divine service approved, used
and observed in the church, and also the word of God,
to acknowledge our own sinfulness unto God, and his
great mercy and goodness unto us, to give thanks unto
Him for His benefits, to make public and common
prayer for all things needful, to visit the sick, to instruct

[1] Strype; *Ecclesiastical Memorials II.* 427.

every man his children and family in virtue and goodness and such other like works". The times for doing
this are the Sunday which has succeeded the Sabbath
"in memory of Christ's resurrection" and "also many
other holy days and festival days, which the Church
hath ordained from time to time". It is pointed out
that these other "holy days" are so called "because
the Church hath ordained that upon those days we
should give ourselves wholly, without any impediment,
unto such holy works as before expressed, whereas
upon other days we may do and apply ourselves to
bodily labour, and be thereby much letted from such
holy and spiritual works".

One or two points may be noted thus far in the
statement. First, the programme for Sunday is such
that if a man strictly observe it he may be expected
to have but little time for ordinary recreation. Apart
from attendance at worship, the visiting of the sick
and the giving and receiving of instruction in 'virtue
and goodness' will occupy a large part of the day. The
ideal set forth is not far, if at all, short of what is
generally attributed to the teaching of a century later.
Secondly, it will be seen that the old custom of holy
days was retained, but an attempt was made to get
away from the superstition which had grown up round
their use and from the abuses which had attached themselves to their observance.

That the authorities responsible for *The King's
Book* did not regard all Sunday work as unlawful is
made clear when they say: "Men must have special care
that they be not over scrupulous or rather superstitious
in abstaining from bodily labour upon the holy day.
For, notwithstanding all that is afore spoken, it is not
meant but we may, upon the holy day, give ourselves
to labour for the speedy performance of the necessary
affairs of the prince and the commonwealth, at the
commandment of them that have rule and authority
therein. And also in all other times of necessity, as for

saving of our corn and cattle, when it is like to be in danger, or like to be destroyed, if remedy be not had in time". "The holy day" here, as in other statements of this early period of the Reformation, includes Sundays as well as Church festival days.

On the other hand, there is nothing in the document to sanction Sunday amusements, but rather they are definitely forbidden. For the statement says that those who do not worship and exercise the holy works appointed for the day but "as commonly is used, pass the time either in idleness, in gluttony, in riot, or other vain or idle pastime, do break this commandment". Indeed, it says that such people "should be better occupied labouring in their fields, and to be kept at plough, than to be idle at home. And women should better bestow their time in spinning of wool, than upon the Sabbath day to lose their time in leaping and dancing, and other idle wantonness". [1] This last statement is of the greatest importance and significance. The early Reformation position in England was evidently that the Sunday must be passed first and foremost in worship and the exercise of good works and secondly, if necessary, in ordinary work, but no sanction was given to the use of any part of the day for recreation.

Here is the first break with the old traditions. The inclusion of the phrase 'as is commonly used' in reference to the passing of the day in 'vain or idle pastime' bears out what has been already noted about the pre-Reformation Sunday. The old liberty of the people, or 'licence' if that word be preferred, to amuse themselves on the Sunday is ended, in theory at any rate. But this is not all, for the time which may not now be used for recreation is to be used for work. Had it been possible to enforce the idea behind this document it seems that the English Sunday would have been a

[1] *Formularies of Faith put forth by Authority during the reign of Henry VIII.* Oxford edit. MDCCCXXV. pp. 142-148.

grimmer thing than even the caricature known so often as the 'Puritan Sunday'.

This idea that Sunday labour was quite permissible once the duties of worship were discharged was common with the early Reformers. John Frith for example, in his Declaration of Baptism, in a reference to the way Sunday should be observed says that such days "were instituted that the people should come together to hear God's word, receive the sacraments, and give God thanks. That done, they may return unto their houses, and do their business as well as any other day. He that thinketh that a man sinneth which worketh on the holy day, if he be weak or ignorant, ought better to be instructed, and so to leave his hold".[1]

[1] *Works of Tyndale and Frith*, edited T. Russell, vol. III, p. 295.

CHAPTER II

It is customary to think of the reign of Edward VI as the period of the doctrinal as distinct from the political Reformation in this country. We should expect, therefore, that the doctrine of the nature and use of the Sunday would receive attention in this reign, and we should expect that the man whose name is pre-eminently associated with the establishment of the Protestant position in doctrine would not neglect to define his views on the question of Sunday. Thomas Cranmer, right at the beginning of the reign, in his Injunctions to the clergy and laity sets out the Protestant position as it was intended that it should be accepted in this country.

First of all it is clear that the accepted usage on the Sunday is displeasing to the Reformers. One would judge that the instructions of Henry VIII on the observance of Sunday had had little or no effect, for the Injunctions say that "in our time God is more offended than pleased, more dishonoured than honoured upon the holy day, because of idleness, pride, drunkenness, quarrelling and brawling, which are most used in such days, people nevertheless persuading themselves sufficiently to honour God on that day, if they hear mass and service, though they understand nothing to their edifying". For the future, therefore, the King commands his subjects to keep the Sunday "in hearing the word of God read and taught, in private and public prayers, in knowledging their offences to God, and amendment of the same, in reconciling themselves

charitably to their neighbours where displeasure hath
been, in oftentimes receiving the communion of the very
body and blood of Christ, in visiting of the poor and
sick, in using all soberness and godly conversation".
It is again felt necessary to point out the fact that all
Sunday labour is not unlawful for the Injunction says
that "all parsons, vicars, and curates shall teach and
declare unto their parishioners, that they may with a
safe and quiet conscience, in the time of harvest, labour
upon the holy and festival days, and save that thing
which God hath sent. And if for any scrupulosity, or
grudge of conscience, men should superstitiously abstain from working upon those days, that then they
should grievously offend and displease God".[1]

Elsewhere in his writings Cranmer explains his views
on the meaning to be attached to Sunday observance.
He says: "There be two parts of the Sabbath day: one
is the outward bodily rest from all manner of labour
and work; and this is mere ceremonial, and was taken
away, with other sacrifices and ceremonies, by Christ
at the preaching of the Gospel. The other part of the
Sabbath-day is the inward rest, or ceasing from sin. . . .
This spiritual Sabbath, that is, to abstain from sin, and
to do good, are all men bound to keep all the days of
their life, and not only on the Sabbath day".[2] What
he terms 'the ceremonial part of the sabbath' having
gone, the Church has substituted for it the Sunday with
the implication that the requirements of the day are
those set out by the demands of the Church.

The official idea of the observance of Sunday was
further set forth in an Act of 1552. This says that it is
necessary "that there should be some certain Times
and Days appointed wherein the Christian should cease
from all other kinds of Labours, and should apply
themselves only and wholly unto . . . holy works
properly pertaining unto true Religion" and as it is the

[1] *Remains of Thomas Cranmer*, Vol. IV, p. 336.
[2] Ditto, p. 232.

duty of the Church to appoint the time and number of
such days, this is done by this act. The list of days
includes all the Sundays of the year and a certain
number of Saints' days. But once again the fear that
people will take advantage of this Act and refuse to
perform any work on the Sunday is seen and so the
statute enacts "That it shall be lawful to every Hus-
bandman, Labourer, Fisherman, and to all and every
other person or persons of what estate, degree or condition he or they be, upon the Holy-days aforesaid, in
Harvest, or at any other time in the year when necessity shall require, to labour, ride, fish or work any kind
of work, at their free wills and pleasure".[1] This would
seem to provide a fair scope for any who desired to work
upon the Sunday to do so, seeing that they themselves
were apparently to be the judges of the necessity of
such work.

The unsatisfactory position of prohibiting amusements but permitting work upon the Sunday seems to
have been apparent to some of the Reformers. Thomas
Becon, chaplain to Cranmer, seems to have been more
clear upon this point than his Archbishop was. In discussing what it is to sanctify the Sunday he says that
to do so is "Not to spend that day idly in wicked
pastimes, banquetting, carding, dancing, pleasures of
the flesh, etc; nor yet in bargaining, buying and selling,
as they do which run to fairs and markets on the
Sabbath-day; but . . . the mind utterly sequestered
from all worldly things, and the body free from all
servile words, to address ourselves, and to apply our
whole mind and body unto godly and spiritual
exercises".[2]

John Hooper, too, is clear that the Sunday should be
a day of rest from ordinary labour. He plainly sets out
the duty of the master to see that his servants are
exempt from Sunday work with the complementary

[1] 5 and 6 Edward VI.
[2] *Writings of the Rev. Thomas Becon*, p. 416.

duty of seeing "that they exercise themselves upon the Sabbath in hearing the word of God". " If," says Hooper, "man, and beast that is man's servant, should without repose and rest always labour, they might never endure the travail of the earth. God, therefore, as he that intendeth the conservation and wealth of man and the thing created to man's use, commandeth this rest and repose from labour, that his creature may indure and serve as well their own necessary affairs and business, as preserve the youth and offspring of man and beast". This emphasis upon the privilege and duty of rest on Sunday as well as of worship seems, as we have seen, to have been needed, the duty having been ignored or but slightly dwelt on by previous teachers. Hooper, as might be expected, has no sanction to give to Sunday amusements or Sunday trading for "not to cease from doing of ill, but to abuse the rest and ease of the Sabbath in sports, games, and pastimes, keeping of markets and fairs upon the Sabbath, is to abuse the Sabbath".[1]

It is difficult to obtain much direct evidence as to the way the ordinary people observed the Sunday at this period as distinct from the precepts and ordinances of individuals and the State as to how they *ought* to observe it. But as far as any definite conclusion is warranted, it seems to be that little or no actual change took place. The people attended service, as they had always done. The Act of Uniformity in 1552 made attendance at the Parish Church compulsory, it having been found that numbers of people were absenting themselves from worship. At the service, of course, they would find startling alterations. The service was now in English, following the publication of the first English Prayer Book in 1549. Some of the clergy were not wearing the customary vestments, many of the images and relics had disappeared from their accustomed places in the church, and a communion table had

been substituted for the altar in some of the churches.
Men capable of preaching were hard to find and Cranmer, in the Injunctions already referred to, stipulated a
minimum of one sermon every quarter of the year.
But when there was no sermon the clergy were to
"openly and plainly recite to their parishioners in the
pulpit the Pater Noster, the Credo, and Ten Commandments in English, to the intent the people may learn
the same by heart: exhorting all parents and house-
holders to teach their children and servants the same,
as they are bound by the law of God and in conscience
to do". [1]

Service over, and the discussions, occasioned by the
changes and innovations just referred to, ended, the
people probably passed their time much as they had
done in pre-Reformation days. That the playing of
games and the holding of fairs and markets had not
ceased is shown by the references to such things in the
writings of men like Cranmer, Becon and Hooper.
Working on the Sunday was certainly not unheard of,
although some had doubts as to its legitimacy. In 1549
the Bailiffs and Burgesses of Aldeburgh in Suffolk said
that nobody must go to sea "on any Sunday between
St. Martin and Twelfth Day before twelve o'clock or be
driving of sprats upon any Saturday after eight o'clock
in the afternoon". But although forty-three inhabitants subscribed this order a marginal note queries the
legality of it as being "against the profit of the common
people". [2] In the same year we read: "The fourth day
of August, the which was Sunday, was men set at work
from Newgate all along by the city walls to pull down
the gardens that was made along by the walls of the
city with houses". [3] This, one would have thought,
hardly came within the category of works of necessity
In the next year some attempt was made to regulate
Sunday trading, but only during the actual times of

[1] *Remains of Thomas Cranmer*, Vol. IV, p. 329.
[2] *Historical Manuscripts Commission*, Fifteenth Report, Appendix, p. 281.
[3] *Chronicle of the Grey Friars*, edited J. G. Nichols, p. 61.

Divine Service. "This year the fourteenth day of November was proclaimed through all London that no victuallers nor taverns should keep no resort of people in their houses for victuals on the Sundays nor holy days till all services were done, and that should be at eleven the clock; and also at afternoon till evensong were done, in pain of great imprisonment at the king's commandment".[1] Sunday was still a day on which the State might mete out punishment to evil-doers, for we read of two servants who were beaten with rods at a pillar in Cheapside on June 1st, 1553, "and on the morrow after, which was the Sunday, and then was two others in the same case beaten at the same pillar".[2]

As in so much of the Protestantism of Edward VI's reign, therefore, it would seem that theory was in advance of actual practice in the matter of Sunday observance. In the matter of theory too, as we have seen, uniformity had not been attained. But it is clear that the theory of the Protestant Sunday was in several ways quite different from the theory of the Roman Catholic Sunday. We shall expect, therefore, when we come to the reign of Elizabeth, to see some determined attempt to make practice more nearly conform with this Protestant theory. In the meantime, the interlude of Mary's reign with its restoration of Roman Catholicism will concern us but little. The act of Edward VI's reign, which we have noted as dealing officially with the question of Sunday observance, was repealed, and Sunday games and amusements were resumed if indeed, as we have questioned, they had ever ceased. We read that on a Sunday in October, 1554, "the King and Queen danced together, there being a brave maskery at Court" and that on another Sunday there was "a bear-baiting on the Bankside".[3] There is one unexpected and apparently inexplicable exception to the general resumption of that freedom to spend the Sunday

[1] *Chronicle of the Grey Friars*, p. 68.
[2] Ditto, p. 78.
[3] Strype: *Ecclesiastical Memorials*, Vol. V, pp. 319 and 327, edition of MDCCCXXII.

as one wished once the necessary attendance at church had been made. This was at Canterbury where, in 1554-5, as the editors of the Ninth Report of the *Historical Manuscripts Commission* say: "Sabbath-breaking was for the first time made a penal offence, an innovation more characteristic of the Puritan times of Elizabeth than of the Catholic of Mary".[1]

[1] *Historical Manuscripts Commission*, Ninth Report, p. 155.

CHAPTER III

THE OFFICIAL ATTITUDE OF CHURCH AND STATE ON THE SUNDAY QUESTION IN ELIZABETH'S REIGN

ELIZABETH'S attitude to the subject of Sunday observance was in line with the whole of her religious policy—it was in the nature of a compromise between the extreme Protestant view and the Roman Catholic view. Everyone must attend church on the Sunday because it was right and proper that they should, and indeed an unheard of thing that they should not, and because only so could Elizabeth be sure that all conformed to the system of worship ordained by the State. But that duty discharged Elizabeth would seem to have been content herself to allow the people to pass their time as they wished. The Act of Uniformity of 1558 ensured amongst other things that everyone attended his or her Parish Church on the Sunday, the penalty for not doing so being a fine of twelve pence. This provision was detailed more exactly in the Injunctions issued by the Queen in the following year. [1] The statement there made with regard to a person's duty on the Sunday follows almost word for word the statement made in the Injunctions of Edward VI's reign which have been referred to in the previous chapter. There is the same permission given for work in harvest time. In 1560 Archbishop Parker inquired among his metropolitan visitation queries: "Whether be in your parishes any inn-keeper or ale-wives, that admit any resort to their houses in time of common prayer; any that commonly absent themselves from their own church, or otherwise

[1] Wilkins; *Concilia*, Vol. IV, p. 184.

idly or lewdly profaneth the Sabbath day".[1] That is to say, except for the very vague reference to a general profanation of the Sunday, all that is desired is that there be nothing to hinder the attendance of all at the Parish Church in the time of Divine Worship. There is an indication that many of the clergy would have preferred stricter regulations, for, as one writer on the subject has said, the Convocation of 1562 "are believed to have originated a bill for the postponing such fairs and markets as fell on a Sunday to the next working day, which was twice read, but by Elizabeth's influence was thrown out".[2] That the feeling of the House of Commons was also in favour of a stricter Sunday observance is seen in a draft of a bill printed by Strype in the documents appended to his life of Grindal. He gives the document no date but as he gives in his *Annals*[3] under the year 1566 the fact that such a bill was twice read in that year it seems probable that 1566 is the date. No such bill became law but the terms of it are interesting as reflecting the thoughts of many of the members of Parliament at that time. Its first provision was to ensure that where markets and fairs were customarily held on the Sunday (another proof if one were needed that they were still so held) they should in future be held on the Saturday or the Monday. It also would have prevented the opening of any shop until after service time was over and would have prevented servants from being made to work unnecessarily on the Sunday. That such points were embodied in the bill shows us that shops did open all day on Sunday and that much unnecessary work was done. It wisely said, too, that all "cases of necessity" were to be determined by the clergymen or a magistrate and not solely by the conscience of the employer.[4] We can imagine that such

[1] Strype's *Life of Parker*, Vol. III, p. 31, edit. MDCCCXXI.
[2] E. V. Neale: *Feasts and Fasts*, p. 189; see also E. Gibson; *Codex Juris I*, 236 and 242.
[3] Strype's *Annals*, Vol. I. Part 2., p. 238, edit. MDCCCXXIV. See also Gibson: *Codex Juris I*, 242.
[4] Strype: *Grindal*, p. 478 edit. of MDCCCXXI.

a bill would not be in accord with the royal will and that it was withdrawn by royal command. At any rate nothing more seems to have been heard of it.

There is no doubt at all that Elizabeth herself was fully in sympathy with the idea of her people amusing themselves by means of the recognized sports and games after church hours on Sunday. In 1569 Elizabeth gave a license to a man named Powlter to organize Sunday games. This document gives an interesting picture of the times as well as revealing the attitude of the Queen and is worth reproducing in its essential features. It is directed to the mayors, sheriffs and other responsible officers of Middlesex and says:—"Whereas we are informed that one John Seconton Powlter, dwelling within the parish of St. Clement Danes, being a poor man, having four small children, and fallen into decay, is licensed to have and use some plays and games at or upon nine several Sundays for his better relief, comfort and sustentation within the county of Middlesex, to commence and begin at and from the 22nd day of May next coming after the date hereof, and not to remain in one place not above three several Sundays, and we considering that great resort of people is like to come thereunto, we will and require you as well for good order, as also for the preservation of the Queen's majesty's peace, that you take with you four or five of the discreet and substantial men within your office or liberties, where the games shall be put in practise, then and there to foresee and do your endeavours to your best, in that behalf during the continuance of the games or plays which games are hereafter severally mentioned, that is to say; the shooting with the standard, the shooting with the broad arrow, the shooting at the twelve skore prick (target) the shooting at the Turk, the leaping for men, the running for men, the wrestling, the throwing of the sledge, and the pitching of the bar, with all such other games as have at any time heretofore or now be licensed used or played. Given the 26th day of April in the eleventh year of the Queen's majesty's reign".[1]

The precautions to be taken by the officers to whom this document was addressed resemble the special police attendance at some sports' meeting at the present time. But just as every Saturday now many football or cricket matches and other games take place without the presence of any police because the games are not calculated to draw large crowds of spectators, so we may picture people playing on the village green or in the market square or other open space on any Sunday in the early part of Elizabeth's reign, once Divine Service was over, without interference from the authorities.

The next important document to consider is the *Homily of the Place and Time of Prayer* issued in 1574. In the sense that this was a statement appointed to be read in the churches it is an authoritative statement but it is questionable whether it reflected the mind of all the officials of the Church and we may assume that it went somewhat further than the Queen's own private opinion in the direction of a stricter observance of the Sunday. The Homily shows that the way in which Sunday was kept did not meet with the approval of those responsible for drawing up the statement. Here again, making allowance of course for the, perhaps unconscious, over-emphasis of the cleric zealous for a more godly mode of life, there is presented a vivid picture of the attitude towards the Sunday adopted by many of the people. The Homily says: "It is lamentable to see the wicked boldness of those that will be counted God's people, who pass nothing at all of keeping and hallowing the Sunday. And these people are of two sorts. The one sort, if they have any business to do, though there be no extreme need, they must not spare for the Sunday, they must ride and journey on the Sunday; they must drive and carry on the Sunday; they must row and ferry on the Sunday; they must buy

[1] Wilkins: *Concilia*, Vol. IV, p. 255.

and sell on the Sunday; they must keep markets and fairs on the Sunday. Finally, they use all days alike, work-days and holy days all are one. The other sort is worse. For although they will not travel nor labour on the Sunday, as they do on the week-day; yet they will not rest in holiness, as God commandeth; but they rest in ungodliness and filthiness, prancing in their pride, pranking and pricking, pointing and painting themselves, to be gorgeous and gay; they rest in excess and superfluity, in gluttony and drunkenness, like rats and swine; they rest in brawling and railing, in quarrelling and fighting: they rest in wantonness, in toyish talking, in filthy fleshliness; so that it doth too evidently appear that God is more dishonoured, and the devil better served on the Sunday than upon all the days in the week beside ".[1]

The language of this statement is hardly less severe than that usually attributed to the strictest sect of that branch of the Puritans who would have imposed a multiplicity of moral regulations upon the people. Yet it was not such a Puritan blast but a carefully prepared presentation of the views of the authorities of the State Church. If this is realized it will make it all the easier to understand why it was that there was, as we shall see later, a growing movement in the country in the direction of a reform of the methods of keeping the Sunday. It will be observed, too, that those responsible for the Homily, while they disapprove of work upon the Sunday, censure more severely those who idle away the day. Their experience taught them that if some people pleased themselves as to the way they spent their free time upon the Sunday, their pleasure took forms which were a nuisance and a danger to peaceful citizens. In view of what they were bound to regard as a very unsatisfactory attitude towards the keeping of the Sunday, the authorities responsible for the Homily set out their conclusions as to the manner in which the day

[1] *Homily of the Place and Time of Prayer*, edit. MDCCCL, pp. 341-352.

should be observed. Here their language is not quite so clear—a proof that opinion as to the right way of spending the day was still in a state of flux. They are quite clear that the chief duty of everyone is to worship in the church on the Sunday. In fact the emphasis put upon that suggests that they were somewhat alarmed by the neglect of many people even to observe that long established custom. They repudiate, too, as do all the early Protestants, any obligation to observe in any sense of the word the old Jewish Sabbath. Yet they have come to realize, as we have seen, that rest was a necessity on the Sunday and they base the obligation to rest upon what they term 'the law of nature'. Thus they say: "Whatsoever is found in the commandment (i.e. the Fourth Commandment) appertaining to the law of nature, as a thing most godly, most just, and needful for the setting forth of God's glory, it ought to be retained and kept of all good Christian people. And, therefore, by this commandment, we ought to have a time, as one day in the week, wherein we ought to rest, yea, from our lawful and needful works. . . . God's people should use the Sunday holily, and rest from their common and daily business, and also give themselves wholly to heavenly exercises of God's true religion and service".[1]

But even if Elizabeth was at one with those responsible for framing the Homily on the matter of attendance at church her practice differed from this theory in the matter of work on the Sunday. It seems to have been quite a regular thing for the Council to meet to transact all kinds of business on Sunday. Ambassadors from foreign courts were frequently granted an audience on that day.[2] Clearly the Queen felt that once the duty of Divine Worship had been satisfactorily attended to it was permissible to spend the remainder of the day in work or amusement as

[1] *Homily of the Place and Time of Prayer*, edit. MDCCCL, pp. 341-352.
[2] *Journal of Sir Francis Walsingham* 1570-1593, edit. C. T. Martin, pp. 16, 17, 18, 20, 21 and other references.

seemed needful or attractive. In this matter, as in many things connected with the realm of religion, Elizabeth held views which, as her reign progressed, were more and more divergent from those of an increasing number of her subjects and even of Parliament and her advisers. A Mr. Fuller, in 1586, was very outspoken on the attitude of Elizabeth herself. He said: "I fear, O gracious sovereign, that your Majesty hath too little used so to sanctify the Lord's Sabbaths; for if you had, things could never have gone on as now they do; and how do your Majesty's people sanctify it? How? Alas, alas, they (by all likelihoods) do without punishment offend God more at that day than in any other day in the week".[1]

Elizabeth, and consequently her Council and Parliament, did very little officially to change the existing law. There were times however when even Elizabeth was forced to act. One of these occasions would seem to have been in 1580 when the magistrates of the City of London obtained a decree from the Queen forbidding the performance of plays and interludes on Sunday within the City.[2] In the following year the Council agreed, upon the suggestion of the Bishop of Chester, to refer to Parliament the matter of the proposed prohibition of fairs on Sundays and of trading before morning prayers.[3] If this were ever done it seems to have escaped record. In that year however Parliament did pass an act which once again enacted that all must attend their Parish Church on the Sunday.[4] The motive for this was the spread of Roman Catholic teaching in the country and the determination to prevent people from absenting themselves from church for religious scruples.

Sir Simond D'Ewes mentions that Parliament had under consideration in 1585 a Bill for the better obser-

[1] *The Seconde Parte of a Register*, edit. A. Peel, p. 54: Original MSS., p. 300.
[2] William Prynne: *Histrio-Mastix*, p. 4911 and Heylyn: *History of the Sabbath Book II*, p. 249.
[3] W. H. Frere: *The English Church in the reign of Elizabeth and James I*, p. 197.
[4] Act of 1581.

vation of the Sunday. It was apparently debated for
several days and only just passed both Houses of
Parliament, and the Queen refused her approval to
it.[1] In 1601 Parliament tried again. On December
11th a Bill was passed by the House of Commons prohibiting fairs and markets on Sunday.[2] But nothing
more is heard of it. The next day the House of Commons had before it for the third reading a Bill to enforce a more regular attendance at church on Sundays.
This seems to have aroused considerable discussion and
was opposed by some as needless and a reflection upon
the power of the clergy in that it presupposed the
imposition of a fine to be more efficacious than the
exhortation of the minister. Others thought it un-
workable. Eventually it was lost by one vote.[3] Thus
officially matters stood very much as they had done at
the beginning of the Reformation period. When Elizabeth died it was still permissible, provided you had
attended church, to play certain games or even to work
upon the Sunday. But many were feeling that the official attitude was not the right one and some were
attempting in their own way to modify or change existing customs.

[1] Simond D'Ewes: *Complete Journal*, p. 322.
[2] *Cal State Papers Dom* 1601, Vol. CCLXXXIII No. 12.
[3] *Cal State Papers Dom* 1601, Vol. CCLXXXIII No. 16 and D'Ewes, pp. 682-3.

CHAPTER IV

THE ACTUAL OBSERVANCE OF SUNDAY AND THE
ATTEMPTS OF LOCAL AUTHORITIES TO REGULATE THAT
OBSERVANCE DURING ELIZABETH'S REIGN

A VERY good picture of the way Sunday was spent in
the City of London and its environs early in Elizabeth's
reign may be obtained from the diary of Henry
Machyn. Machyn was what we should term to-day an
undertaker whose diary, apart from recording matters
of his business, contains many interesting references to
everyday events which he witnessed or of which he
heard. He tells us that on a Sunday in June 1559 a
May-game was played before the Queen and her
Council at Greenwich.[1] On Sunday, August 27th in
the same year at Finsbury the Lord Mayor and Aldermen were present at shooting contests and other
games.[2] There were jousts[3] at the royal palace on
Sunday, November 5th, 1559 and a play[4] before the
Queen on Sunday, December 31st. On Sunday, April
21st, 1560, Machyn refers to the sermon preached at
Paul's Cross before the Lord Mayor and Aldermen and
a large audience. Preaching was a rarity and the
preaching at Paul's Cross was often well attended
even though complaint might be made of the attendance
at the churches. The same afternoon the diarist
describes further jousts at the Court.[5] A very similar
account is given for the following Sunday.[6] On Sunday,

[1] *Diary of Henry Machyn*, edit. J. G. Nichols, p. 201.
[2] Ditto, p. 207.
[3] Ditto, p. 216.
[4] Ditto, p. 221.
[5] Ditto, pp. 231-2.
[6] Ditto, p. 233.

3

February 1st, 1562, at night there "was the goodliest maske came out of London that ever was seen" which proceeded to the Court to perform there.[1] The entry for Sunday, November 8th, 1562, describes the state progress of Elizabeth from Hampden Court to Somerset Place.[2] One would gather therefore that there was usually no lack of entertainment for the citizens of London upon the Sunday early in Elizabeth's reign.

After all the religious changes of the previous thirty years it is not surprising that many of the people early in Elizabeth's reign were without much religious conviction. Many of these people, left to their own devices for a great part of the Sunday, did not know how well to spend their time. It was a rough age and men gave free rein to their passions all too easily. It is not surprising therefore to find many complaints about the way the Sunday was spent. A preacher at Blandford in 1570 denounced the attitude of many to the Sunday saying: "the multitude call (it) their revelling day: which day is spent in bull-baitings, bear-baitings, bowlings, dicing, carding, dancing, drunkenness and whoredom."[3] John Stockwood, preaching at Paul's Cross in 1578 is reported as saying: "Will not a filthy play, with the blast of a trumpet, sooner call thither a thousand, than an hour's tolling of a bell bring to the Sermon a hundred . . .? If you resort to the Theatre, the Curtain, or other places of Playe in the city, you shall on the Lord's day have these places, with many other that I cannot reckon, so full, as possible they can throng." He adds that in some places the players "shame not in the time of divine service to come and dance about the church."[4] In 1580 there was a bad earthquake shock in London and other parts of the country and the Church authorities appointed special prayers to be said to avert the wrath of God and an

[1] *Diary of Henry Machyn*, edit. J. G. Nichols, p. 276.
[2] Ditto, p. 295.
[3] J. Brand: *Popular Antiquities of Great Britain I*, p. 158.
[4] Stephen Gosson: *School of Abuse*, edit. E. Arber, p. 9.

admonition was drawn up which the clergy were to read to their congregations. This enumerates the sins and shortcomings of the people and refers to the fact that the Sunday "is spent full heathenishly in taverning, tippling, gaming, playing, and beholding of bearbaiting and stage-plays; to the utter dishonour of God, impeachment of all godliness, and unnecessary consuming of men's substances, which ought to be better employed. The want of orderly discipline and catechising hath either sent great numbers, both old and young, back again into papistry, or let them run loose into godless atheism."[1] The State by its vigilance aided by the memory of the Marian persecutions prevented any possibility of a return to papistry. But it was not in a position to prevent the danger of a "godless atheism".

There was a tremendous need at the beginning of Elizabeth's reign for the people to be instructed in true religion. The mere enforcement of attendance at worship, even though the service was in English, was insufficient. The people needed educating in the truths and ways of religion. This could only be done satisfactorily through the medium of preaching, but men capable of teaching the people in that way were woefully lacking. Reference has already been made to the infrequency of sermons due to the inability to find qualified preachers. Without qualified preachers the sermon was either a farce or a danger. Strype, writing of the early years of Elizabeth's reign, says: "It was commonly said even in these times, but chiefly by the enemies of the gospel, 'What should I do at a sermon? I know as much before I go in as I shall learn there. I can read the scripture at home, and comfort myself sufficiently.'"[2] These words have a distinctly modern ring about them. The speaker of them would inm any cases have much more justification for using them in

[1] Strype: *Annals*, Vol. II. Part 2, p. 397.
[2] Strype: *Annals*, Vol. I. Part 1, p. 272.

the early years of Elizabeth's reign than any user of them to-day. Consequently it happened that often the good preachers lacked an audience and had to say: "Come into a church the Sabbath day, and ye shall see but few, though there be a sermon; but the alehouse is ever full." [1]

A modern writer on the state of the English Church in the early years of Elizabeth's reign has shown the very unsatisfactory state of conditions then prevailing. "Official documents, beginning with the archdeacons' records of 1560 and extending down to these returns of 1563, show a great lack of clergy, a number of vacant livings and ruinous churches, and an amount of absenteeism and other disorders which is very painful; but such things are clearly not the sudden result of the recent changes but the accumulating consequences of a long chain of causes." [2] Because they were not of sudden but of slow growth these conditions meant that the people were very ignorant of spiritual truths. The same writer shows that out of eighty-seven clergy in the diocese of London only thirty-one could preach. Thus it is no wonder that some people had a very low idea of the sanctity of the Sunday. They would turn with relief from the barrenness of the obligatory service to the freedom of their own devices, even though in some cases those devices were not calculated to benefit them morally. It must not be assumed, of course, that by any means all the people, or even a majority of them, sought depraved means of relaxation. There must have been many who spent the Sunday quietly in their homes, or in forms of amusement which at any rate were harmless to others. But in many places there were a number of those whose conduct was a nuisance if not a danger to others until steps had to be taken to restrain their wildness.

It has been seen in the previous chapter that Eliza-

---

[1] Strype: *Annals*, Vol. I. Part 1, p. 270.
[2] W. H. Frere: *The English Church in the reign of Elizabeth and James I*, p. 104.

beth, and consequently her advisers, did little to regulate the way in which Sunday should be spent, other than to enforce attendance at church. But it must be remembered that the Elizabethan age was one which witnessed great activity on the part of the local justices of the peace. Many were the duties which devolved upon them, and which seem to have been very conscientiously fulfilled. They were, in many cases, no doubt because they were brought closely into contact with the actual instances of abuse, desirous of regulating the way the Sunday was spent. Those who moved almost exclusively in Court circles, and particularly the Queen herself, might from their personal experience find little cause for complaint in the jousts and plays and dances which filled that part of the Sunday which was not spent in religious devotions. If they had no religious scruples upon the matter they probably were not made aware of any moral danger or personal inconvenience. The magistrates, on the other hand, who had to deal with cases of drunkenness or brawling or immorality, caused by the license of the Sunday, felt otherwise on the matter. The same was true of many of those responsible for the good government of the towns. One instance, that of the City of London obtaining a decree against the Sunday performance of plays in 1580, has already been noticed. Several other cases of the action of local authorities may now be taken.

In 1572 at Ipswich an order was made by the town authorities that no shops should be opened for the purpose of selling any goods at any time on Sunday. The only persons exempted from the regulation were the butchers, and they were not to open during the hours of service.[1] In 1576 the Rochester records of the Admiralty Court show the presentment of a certain Thomas Herring "for working with his lighter upon the Sabbath day".[2]

[1] *Historical Manuscripts Commissions*, Ninth Report, p. 254.
[2] Ditto, p. 289.

On April 21st, 1574, eight of the justices of the peace at Manchester directed that "every church-warden, constable and sworn man shall, every Sunday and holy day, take the names of such persons as do walk in places ordained for divine service, in the time of the sermon or divine service". These names, to-gether with those of people who walk out of church before the end of the service, are to be presented to the justices.[1] This seems to argue a zeal on the part of the magistrates not only to enforce attendance at church as the law directed, but to see that as far as possible all who attended benefited by their presence. There is no doubt that measures were sometimes needed to ensure a peaceable and orderly conduct of worship. Apart from the rougher element which might seize upon any pretext to create a disturbance, there was the possibil-ity of interruption from those who were out of sym-pathy with the order of service established by the State, either on the grounds of their ultra-Protestant or on the grounds of their Roman Catholic sympathies. Strype gives an account of such a disturbance taking place at Norwich in 1572. On that occasion as he says "three or four lewd boys, set on by some lewder persons (whether they were papists or protestants disaffected to the liturgy) came into the church, and as the said minister began to read 'My soul doth magnify the Lord' etc., they burst out into singing of psalms suddenly and unlooked for; and being commanded by the minister to cease, they continued singing, and he reading; so as all was out of order, and the godly, well-disposed auditors there disquieted, and much grieved."[2]

The records of presentments for the parish of Roch-dale in April, 1588, include "Adam Stolte, gentleman, upon the Sabbath day, in the evening, being either the last Sunday in December or the first in January, had a minstrel which played upon a gitterne at his house, with a great number of men and women dancing". At the same time the duties of the jurors for Manchester are given and they include that of presenting those who keep "wakes, fairs, markets, bear-baitings, bull-baitings, greenes, alleys, may-games, piping and dancing, hunting and gaming, upon the Sabbath day."[1] Clearly the local authorities in that part of the country intended to enforce a stricter observance of the Sunday than the law of the land actually laid down.

There is more evidence available for the state of affairs in Lancashire just about this time than for many parts of the country, but there seems no reason to suppose that the abuses there were greater, or the attempts to reform such abuses more zealous, than elsewhere and so it may be assumed that what went on in Lancashire had its counterpart in other places. There is a very interesting document drawn up by fourteen Lanchashire men, probably in 1589, setting out what they term to be "the enormities of the Sabbath" together with their suggestions for the reform of the same. This document says: "The enormities of the Sabbath these:

Wakes, fairs, markets, bear-baiting, bull-baiting, ales, may-games, resorting to alehouses in time of divine service, piping and dancing, hunting, and all manner of unlawful gaming.

The meanes how to reform the same:

To give in charge at the public quarter sessions to all mayors, bailiffs, and constables, and other civil officers, churchwardens, and other officers of the church, to suppress (by) all means lawful the said disorders of the Sabbath, as also to present the said offenders at the Quarter Sessions, that they may be dealt with for the same so far as Law will bear, and for the present time to apprehend the minstrel, bearward and such like chief authors of the said disorders. And then to bring them immediately before some justice of peace to be punished at their discretion."

[1] *Manuscripts of Lord Kenyon*—Historical MSS. Report, p. 382.

They advise also the presentment according to law of all who fail to attend Divine Service and declare that it is necessary "to bind the alehousekeepers by special terms in the conditions of their recognisances for the receiving any that are chief maintainers and partakers of the foresaid disorders of the Sabbath as also for the receiving any body at all into their house, or selling ale or other victualls in time of Divine Service."[1]

There seems to be nothing fanatical about this document and it can only be classed as 'puritan' in the sense that it is drawn up by people who wish to guard the spiritual significance of the Sunday. The authors are not people who are dissatisfied in any way with the established system of worship and it is significant that they appear to believe that the abuses they name can be remedied if resource be had to the local authorities.

Probably in the following year, 1590, a statement was drawn up to be presented to the government on behalf of seventeen of the clergy of the diocese of Chester. Those who signed it included the rectors of Bury, Wigan, Middleton, Radcliffe and Prestwich and the Vicars of Blackburn, Whalley, Rochdale and Warrington. They refer to the "continual recourse of Jesuits and Seminary priests into these parts" and the fact that "popish fasts and festivals (now abrogated in the Church of England) (are) duly observed in all these parts, and that with greater devotion than the Sabbath." They go on to say that "fairs and markets in most towns are usually kept upon the Sabbath; by occasion whereof divine service in the afternoon is greatly neglected" and that "wakes, ales, greenes, May-games, rushbearings, bear-baites, doveales, bonfires, all manner unlawful gaming, piping and dancing and such like, are in all places freely exercised upon the Sabbath. By occasion whereof it cometh to pass that the youth will not by any means be brought to attend the exercise of catechising in the afternoon: neither the people

[1] *The Lancashire Lieutenancy*, edit. John Harland, Part II, pp. 217-220.

to be present at the evening service. So that it were
hard for the Preacher to find a competent congregation
in any church to preach unto." Complaint is made
also of the way in which the service is disturbed by
people going in and out of the church during Divine
Service time and "by the great tumults of the people
remaining in the churchyards, streets, and alehouses
in time of divine service. From whence stones are often
times thrown upon the leads of the church, and many
a clamorous noise and shout given out to the dis-
quieting of the congregation." [1]

It will be noticed here that a connection is traced
between the disorders on the Sunday and the absence
from church on the one hand and the trend of Roman
Catholicism on the other. The two certainly seem to
have a bearing upon one another. We need not necessarily accept the idea that ardent Romanists deliberately
incited the people to disturb the Anglican services and
create disturbances on the Sunday—an idea which
was held at that time and in the next century and by
writers since that time. But we can feel sure that many
people, who objected to the stricter Sunday which
Protestantism seemed to be forcing upon them, would
turn with relief to what they would consider to be the
greater freedom of Roman Catholicism. The older
religious system as we have seen had not for a long time
had much to say against merry-making on the Sunday
once the religious service was over. The laxity of the
general religious life of the country before the Reformation had meant that such religious duties as were
supposed to be performed upon the Sunday had become a mere form. Now the renewed interest in
religious matters for which Protestantism was standing
meant to many the imposition of what they regarded
as irksome burdens. Only those whose spiritual life
had been awakened and quickened by the new outlook
in religion would find any necessity for, or joy in, the

[1] *Chetham Miscellanies*, Vol. V, edit. F. R. Raines, pp. 1-4.

attempt to return to the idea of Sunday as a truly holy
day and not a mere holiday.

Evidently the zeal of the clergy and of some of the
magistrates was insufficient to bring about what might
be regarded as a satisfactory state of affairs in Lancashire.
We find a report being made to the Privy Council in
1591 about the conditions of affairs in Lancashire and
Cheshire. This says that in some cases so few people
attend church that many preachers do not think it
worth while to preach while open markets are held
during service time and the people swarm in the streets
and crowd the alehouses. Cockfights and other games
go on even during service hours. Complaint is made
that some of the coroners and justices do not attend
church regularly.[1] In the last statement lies no doubt
the clue to the prevalence of some at any rate of the
disorder. Where the magistrates were not themselves
convinced of the necessity of improving existing conditions little or nothing was possible or likely to be done
at that time. But further evidence exists to show that
many magistrates did attempt to tackle the problem.
At Ormskirk in 1590 "Ralph Pyke of Eccleston, piper,
bound himself for one year not to play the pipe on
Sundays."[2] In the same year at Preston the presentments include "Christopher Poulton alehousekeeper
permitted a bearbait beside his house on Sunday" and
"Margaret Yat . . . and Constance Eccles . . . spin-
sters, on 12th July 1590, being Sunday at Gosenaigh
carried rushes to the church. And William Craven of
Clitherow, piper, on the same day at Clitherow, piped."[3]
At the Manchester sessions in 1592 the license of an alehousekeeper contained the provision that he was not
to entertain "those who uphold disorders on the Sabbath day as of wakes, fairs, markets, bearbaits, bull-
baits, greens, ales, May-games, hunting, bowling, cock
fighting or such like; nothing to be sold during the time

[1] *Calendar of State Papers.* Domestic Series: Elizabeth: Vol. CCXL. No. 138.
[2] *Lancashire Quarter Sessions Records*, Vol. I, edit. J. Tait, p. 8.
[3] Ditto, p. 11.

of divine service except to travellers and those falling sick."[1] Later in the same year several alehouse-keepers were presented at Manchester for selling ale during service time and another man because he had during service time "in his house various men drinking."[2] At Wigan in 1592 two labourers and a butcher were indicted for playing bowls on Sunday.[3] In Manchester in 1601 a man was charged with baiting an ape on Sunday,[4] and in 1602 at Ormskirk an alehouse-keeper was presented because on a Sunday he "had bowling, carding and dicing at the time of divine service."[5] Other similar instances could be given but probably enough has been set forth to show that by the end of Elizabeth's reign determined attempts were being made in some parts of Lancashire at any rate to remedy the abuses mentioned in the documents drawn up by the laity and clergy in 1589 and 1590. These attempts seem to be the natural outcome of an existing state of affairs which those in authority and indeed most law abiding citizens felt to be unsatisfactory. They may be classed as Puritan in tendency if that word be taken to mean a desire to brace the moral tone of the people which had grown flabby during a long period of religious laxity. So much space has been given to affairs in Lancashire round about 1580 not only because so much evidence exists for that part of the country at that time, but because Lancashire was to figure so prominently in the story of the observance of Sunday, in connection with the publication of what is generally termed the King's Book of Sports in the reign of James I. It will be well when that comes to be considered to have in mind the picture of affairs in Lancashire in the previous reign.

To return now to other instances of action being taken by local authorities on the matter of Sunday

---

[1] *Lancashire Quarter Sessions Records*, Vol. I, edit. J. Tait, pp. 51-52.
[2] Ditto, p. 60.
[3] Ditto, p. 64.
[4] Ditto, p. 101.
[5] Ditto, p. 143.

observance in other parts of the country, there are first of all certain orders of the magistrates in Somersetshire. These all dealt with the suppression of church ales and similar revels in 1594 and 1596.[1] In 1595 an order of the justices for Devonshire declared that "Church or parish ales, revels, May-games, plays, and such other unlawful assemblies of the people of sundry parishes unto one parish on the Sabbath day and other times is a special cause that many disorders, contempts of law and other enormities, are there perpetrated and committed, to the great profanation of the Lord's 'Saboth', the dishonour of Almighty God, increase in bastardy and of dissolute life, and of very many other mischiefs and inconvenience, to the great hurt of the commonwealth." They therefore say that these assemblies must cease on the Sunday and that no drink shall be sold at all on the Sunday. A market which had been held on the Sunday at East Budleigh was also forbidden by their orders.[2] Once more it is the disorderliness and immorality, which seemed to be the natural sequence of a lax theory of the sacredness of the Sunday, which made the magistrates feel that it was necessary to restrain the freedom of the people to do just as they liked upon the Sunday.

A letter from Sir Francis Godolphin to Sir Robert Cecil on April 18th, 1597 shows the action the justices in Cornwall felt it necessary to take. The orders made by the magistrates at Bodmin include one that "Wardens and constables (are) to take special note on the Sabbath day what persons absent themselves from divine service and punish the faulty according to the Statute. Every householder to see that their servants and youths be not permitted to play at unlawful games on the Sabbath days or to frequent alehouses, and that view be taken what riotous or wasteful expenses are used in any tippling house and by whom."[3]

[1] William Prynne: Canterburie's Doome, p. 132.
[2] A. H. A. Hamilton: Quarter Sessions from Elizabeth to Anne, pp. 28-29.
[3] Calendar of Manuscripts of the Marquis of Salisbury, Vol. VII, p. 161.

Turning to the other side of England again there is an order made by the magistrates of Ipswich in 1600 that "no waggoner or common carrier of Ipswich shall work on the Sunday, the order being made "forasmuch as the waggoners and common carriers of this town have and do usually begin to travel towards London every week on the Tuesday with their waggons and carriages and do come out of London on the Friday at afternoon and by most part of the Sabbath day to the great offence of Almighty God, and contrary to the laws of the realm, and to the infamy and slander of this town."[1] It is interesting to notice that the order was made with the consent of two of the waggoners of Ipswich. Perhaps we should not be wrong in interpreting this as a sign that men then as to-day in many cases welcomed the enforcement of a day's rest from labour upon the Sunday. Indeed the question of the right of carriers to travel upon the Sunday had been under discussion for some time. In 1583 the Lord Mayor of London had written to Sir Francis Walsingham asking that the order which prevented carriers from travelling either by pack-horse or cart on Sunday within the City of London might be extended to the suburbs.[2] He encloses a petition which he has received from the company of Innholders of London praying that the carriers may not be permitted to leave London on the Sunday. Perhaps in the last case we may detect some ulterior motive in the request as presumably the presence of the carriers in London over the Sunday would bring increased trade to the innkeeper.

The question of the performance or prohibition of stage plays upon the Sunday was one which engaged the attention of the authorities and the public generally in the last two decades of the sixteenth century. Public opinion seems to have been roused particularly on the subject after an accident at Paris Garden in

[1] *Historical Manuscripts Commission*, Ninth Report, p. 256.
[2] *Calendar of State Papers*: Domestic: Elizabeth: Vol. CLXIV, No. 28.

Southwark in 1583 when a scaffold, carrying many spectators of the entertainment provided on a Sunday, broke, and some people were killed and many injured. The Lord Mayor, in reporting the incident to Lord Burghley, said: "It gives great occasion to acknowledge the hand of God for such abuse of His Sabbath day; and moveth me in conscience to beseech your lordship to give orders for redress of such contempt of God's service."[1] The writer said also that he had consulted with some of the magistrates for the County of Surrey who had expressed themselves zealous to reform the abuses of the Sunday but they felt that they lacked authority. The only action on the matter taken by the State seems to have been to prohibit the acting of plays in London and its vicinity by an order of the Privy Council in 1583.[2] Apparently the order was not strictly enforced for long and in 1587 some of the inhabitants of Southwark complained because performances still took place on Sunday. The Privy Council ordered the magistrates of Surrey and Middlesex to enforce the prohibition of plays upon the Sunday. However, on Sunday, June 11th, 1592 a riot broke out in Southwark for the purpose of rescuing a man who had been committed to the Marshalsea and the Lord Mayor, writing to Lord Burghley on the matter, says that: "the said companies assembled themselves by occasion and pretence of their meeting at a play, which besides the breach of the Sabbath day, giveth opportunity of committing these and such like disorders."[3]

Once more it seems to be that for the purposes of maintaining good order the authorities welcomed a stricter regulation of the way people spent the Sunday. But generally speaking public opinion was too much for them. The ordinary people were bent upon enjoying themselves in what they felt was traditionally the right way.

[1] Strype: *Annals*, Vol. III. Part 1, p. 202.
[2] J. P. Collier: *History of English Dramatic Poetry*, Vol. I, p. 270.
[3] Ditto, p. 271.

It seems, therefore, when we review the situation in Elizabeth's reign, that over the greater part of the country people at the end of her reign were still indulging in the sports and pastimes which their ancestors had enjoyed upon the Sunday at the close of the pre-Reformation period. But at the same time the situation in the country had profoundly altered even from what it had been at the beginning of Elizabeth's reign. There was a growing feeling that all was not well with the customary attitude towards Sunday. Too often people abused their liberty upon that day and this, apart from anything else, was leading, as we have seen, to many people advocating, and where possible enforcing, a stricter control over the habits of the people upon the Sunday. Then, and this will be traced out in some detail in the next chapter, the feeling was growing that the claims of God upon a Christian could not be satisfied by a perfunctory attendance at church and that therefore many of the old, accepted, methods of spending the day were unsuitable and must be superceded or changed. That is to say that, whereas Elizabeth and her Council might still feel that as wide a liberty as possible should be allowed to people on the Sunday, provided always that they attended church, there was a growing body of opinion amongst the rank and file of the nation, clergy and laity alike, which was becoming more and more convinced that too much liberty was in danger of promoting an increase in crime and might indeed be classed in itself as a sin.

CHAPTER V

THE GROWTH OF A NEW THEORY ABOUT THE RIGHT OBSERVANCE OF SUNDAY DURING ELIZABETH'S REIGN

BEFORE considering some of the varying Protestant opinions on the right way of keeping Sunday held during Elizabeth's reign it will be interesting to take notice of an orthodox Roman Catholic statement by a devout member of that church. Laurence Vaux was an Englishman dwelling in a monastery at Louvain who in 1567 wrote a catechism for the use of the scholars in his monastery. In this document he deals as follows with the question of Sunday observance. First of all he shows that Christians observe as a holy day not the Saturday or Jewish Sabbath but the Sunday "in which day Christ our Lord arose from death." This day, together with "all feasts and holy days instituted and commanded by the Church" is to be kept holy or sanctified and "we do sanctify the holy day when we apply ourselves to the worshipping of God. Therefore upon Sundays and holy days we ought to search our conscience, and purge it from sin: we should cry and call unto God for mercy and grace, thanking him for his manifold benefits, bestowed upon us: we ought to have in memory Christ's Passion, Paradise, Hell and Purgatory, so to abstain from sin, and exercise ourselves in things that be godly for our soul's health: as in going to the church, to pray devoutly, reverently to hear Mass, and other Divine service."[1]

Vaux then proceeds, after this positive statement of doctrine, to examine the various ways in which the

[1] L. Vaux s *Catechisme or Christian Doctrine*, edit. T. G. Law, p. 35.

proper observance of Sunday may be spoilt. He
decides that the holy day may be broken in four ways.
The first way is "by servile work". "If upon Sundays
or holy days we work or cause other to work any servile
labour, that properly pertaineth to servants: as plough-
ing, carting, digging, and such like, or do use handy-
crafts; how be it for pity or necessity, some things be
permitted to be done upon holy days: as dressing of
meat, preparing of a medicine, burying the dead, and
such like. Also it is permitted upon holy days, to exercise the liberal sciences, and to dispute, or study, to
sing, or to play upon instruments. And if necessity do
constrain to take a journey upon the holy day, it is
permitted."

The second way in which the day is broken is by
omitting to worship in the recognized way. The third
way is "by unreverence of holy things". This includes
"talking, walking, gazing, or occupying ourselves idly"
when at mass and misusing the church or churchyard.
Finally the day is broken "by plays, pastimes or gaming. If we misspend the holy day in unthrifty games, as
cards and dice for covetousness, or when we should be
at Divine service: or if we use dancing for wantonness,
or if we idly stray about, when we should be at Divine
service: or if we frequent taverns or bowling alleys, or
if we use any unhonest place or company. By these
ways and such like we break the holy day, and so
offend God."

Such a document shows clearly that those who, in this
country, claimed for themselves a freedom to spend the
Sunday just as they liked could not find support for
their demand in Roman Catholic theory whatever justification they might adduce from previous Roman
Catholic practice. It shows, too, that in many points
there was a great similarity between the demands which
were now being advanced by the stricter Protestant
thinkers and the views of the Roman Catholic Church.
That is to say with the deepening of religious life in the

Roman Catholic Church as in the Protestant Churches at the end of the sixteenth century there was the accompanying conviction that the Sunday was a day which must in a very especial sense be set apart from the other days of the week. It will be noticed that Vaux does not condemn the playing of all games on the Sunday. Generally speaking it may be said that he makes a distinction between games which afford pure enjoyment to the individuals indulging in them and which cause no harm to others and pastimes which are in themselves incentives to or pretexts for vice or impurity. The former he would allow: the latter he must of necessity condemn. Herein he is in line with the motives which, as we have seen, influenced the magistrates and others in England who felt constrained during Elizabeth's reign to modify and restrain the existing freedom of conduct on the Sunday. In this too, and in his condemnation of any form of servile work he goes further than the official position of the English Church and State as set out in the Injunctions of 1559 and reflected, as we have traced out, in the attitude of the Queen and her advisers during her reign. It would seem, therefore, that the official policy of England with regard to the keeping of Sunday was in Elizabeth's reign lagging behind the more enlightened Roman Catholic teaching and it is therefore small wonder that many of Elizabeth's subjects were dissatisfied with that policy.

The thoughts on the subject of a sound Protestant, although one who in many of his ideas was too liberal to be classed as a Puritan in any narrow sense of the word, about the year 1577 are expressed in a treatise written by John Northbrooke. He considers that the Sunday is appointed for the reading and hearing of the Scriptures; for attending public and private devotions; for alms-giving to the poor; and for visiting the poor and settling differences with one's neighbours. He says: "I do allow of honest, moderate, and good lawful active exercises for recreation, and quickening of our

dull minds" but such pastimes and games as are
indulged in are to be used like sleep to refresh after "we
have laboured enough in weighty matters and serious
affairs".[1] It is quite clear that a mere perfunctory
attendance at one or even two services would not be
considered by Northbrooke as qualifying the individual
for indulgence in sport for the remainder of the day.
Northbrooke would permit the gathering of corn or hay
"which hath been abroad a long time, and to save it"
on the Sunday. This again is a much more guarded
statement than the vague permission for labour in
harvest-time which the Injunctions gave.[2] The individual self-discipline which is implied in Northbrooke's
scheme both for the serious part of the day's activity
and for the recreative part was a virtue few of the
ordinary people at that time were educated to practise.
It would be a tremendous national asset if the people
could be brought to see the value of imposing upon
themselves some such discipline. At the time it seemed
to many of those who desired such a state of affairs
that the end would only be achieved by State tutelage.

The desire of some people to educate the people with
a higher regard for religious things is seen in the
institution of what were generally termed prophesyings.
These were meetings of the clergy to discuss points of
theology and to train each other in preaching. Archbishop Grindal was very favourable towards them
whereas the Queen was very suspicious of them and
eventually suspended Grindal for not forbidding them.
Better preaching, as has been noticed already, was an
essential if the people were to be awakened to any real
spiritual knowledge. Strype gives an account of the
scheme instituted in Northampton with the consent of
the Bishop of Peterborough and the mayor and justices
of the peace in connection with such prophesyings in
1571.[3]

---

[1] John Northbrooke: *A Treatise against Dicing*, pp. 44-45; 63-4.
[2] Wilkins: *Concilia IV.* 184.
[3] Strype: *Annals*, Vol. II. Part 1, pp. 133-134.

This account throws a light upon the method for spending the devotional part of the Sunday which the authorities of Northampton thought suitable at that time. Every Sunday morning the ordinary service, without sermon, in each Parish Church was to be over by nine o'clock (people began their day early then). The people from the various churches in the town were then to assemble in some one church in which the sermon for the day was to be delivered. Attendance at the sermon was compulsory. After evening prayer every Sunday the young people were to be examined publicly before all the congregation in a portion of Calvin's Catechism. This was to continue for an hour. Once a quarter there was to be a general communion with a sermon in every Parish Church, attendance at which was compulsory. This communion was held in two parts. The first one was for the benefit of servants and officials who would have duties later in the day and was to begin at 5 a.m. and was to last, with an hour's sermon, until 8 a.m. The second was for "masters and dames" and was to begin at 9 a.m. and conclude at 12 noon.

An obvious criticism of the scheme seems to be that apart from anything else it aimed at too drastic a change in the lives of the people. But it is worth remembering that there was a plan for compulsory devotions upon the Sunday drawn up fairly early in Elizabeth's reign by officials of the established church and approved by the local authorities. It does not belong to the period that is generally considered the time of strict Puritan influence.

The prophesyings, from which at Northampton the scheme just outlined had grown, did in time tend in certain places at any rate to foster a presbyterian tendency within the ranks of the clergy. They became eventually illegal but it was found difficult to suppress them altogether. We have the Minute book of one of these groups of presbyterianly-minded ministers who had formed themselves into what was called a classis.

This was a somewhat loosely organized meeting of ministers and others to study the Scripture and exercise control over one another in matters of conduct. The Minute book of the Dedham Classis extends from 1582 to 1589 and shows that during that period the subject of the right conduct of the citizen on the Sunday came up for discussion several times but apparently without any very definite and satisfactory conclusion being reached. [1]

In 1583 an oft quoted book was published, *The Anatomy of the Abuses in England*, by Philip Stubbes. In the book the author makes the following statement about the Sunday. "The Sabbath day, of some is well sanctified, namely in hearing the word of God read, preached, and interpreted in private and public prayers, in singing of Godly psalms, in celebrating the sacraments and in collecting for the poor and indigent which are the true uses and ends whereto the Sabbath was ordained. But other some spend the Sabbath day (for the most part) in frequenting of bawdy stage-plays and interludes, in maintaining Lords of misrule (for so they call a certain kind of play which they use), May-games, Church-ales, feasts, and wakes; in piping, dancing, dicing, carding, bowling, tennis playing; in bear-baiting, cock-fighting, hawking, hunting, and such like; in keeping of fairs and markets on the Sabbath; in keeping courts and leets; in football playing, and such other devilish pastimes; reading of lascivious and wanton books, and an infinite number of such like practices and profane exercises used upon that day whereby the Lord God is dishonoured and his Sabbath violated." [2] Stubbes recognizes that his attitude will be considered "too, too Stoical" because he would prevent people from pleasures for which they consider the day was ordained. Yet it will be realized that his attitude was very similar to that which force of circumstances as

[1] *The Presbyterian Movement illustrated by the Minute Book of the Dedham Classis*, edit. R. G. Usher.
[2] Philip Stubbes's *Anatomy of Abuses*, edit. F. S. Furnivall, p. 136.

well as religious conviction was causing many people in the country to adopt.

In 1585 the question of Sunday observance for a while engaged the attention of the University of Cambridge. The matter seems to have been first raised in a sermon preached there by a certain John Smith, M.A. Smith was examined by the Vice-Chancellor and the Heads of the Colleges because his views had been reported to them as new and unusual. In the examination he admitted that in his sermon he had said: "That the plays at Saturday and Sunday at night were breaches of the Christian Sabbath. On Sunday, for that they were at it before the sun was set. On Saturday, for disabling of their bodies for the Sabbath duties."[1] Smith considered that the Sunday ought to be observed for twenty-four hours but his examiners did not agree with this. Smith considered too that the Sunday was not observed properly when anything was done which was not in itself necessary or religious. His examiners did not agree again, thinking people were free to do as they wished provided that their actions did not hinder religion and were not an offence to others.[2] Here it seems that the University authorities adopted pretty well the official attitude of the Church and State whereas Smith was one of those who felt that attitude to be too lax and too vague. The trouble was that almost every person had his own idea as to what constituted a hindrance to religion and what was an offence to others.

While many complaints were made about the lack of preaching there seems to be evidence that where there were good preachers their work achieved good results, at any rate in the direction of better conduct on the Sunday. There exists a petition sent to the Lord Mayor of London, probably in 1587, on behalf of a Mr. Barber who had been suspended from preaching because he

---

[1] University Register quoted in Strype: *Annals*, Vol. III. Part 1, p. 496.
[2] Ditto, p. 497.

would not conform to the regulations of the State Church. It is signed by 119 people who say: "For whiles pride and idleness (the nurses of all ill rule) are so increased in all sorts of people, and plays, vain spectacles, bear-baitings, dancing schools, fence schools, dicing houses, and so many allurements and rostries of iniquity are maintained; if the faithful, diligent, and earnest preachers of the Word of God should suddenly be restrained and put from their accustomed exercises, so long and with so good success heretofore continued, how can it be but the former prophanations of the Lord's Sabbath will be renewed and the places of sin, which by such preaching began to be made more empty than before . . . will be filled." [1]

Strype gives a petition consisting of thirty-four articles which was drawn up to be presented to Elizabeth and Parliament asking among other things for a learned ministry able to preach and resident in the parishes. The thirtieth article deals with the matter of Sunday and begs: "That the Lord's day, even the Sabbath day, which we do barbarously call Sunday, may hereafter be kept so holily, that it be not abused, nor misspent, neither in open feasting, nor in making or using any public shows, plays, or pastimes. Nor that there be any fairs or markets kept upon any Sabbath day hereafter. But that if any fairs or markets hath been heretofore ordained to be kept upon a Sabbath day, either it may be put off to be kept within the next two days after the said Sabbath day; or if, by the long accustomed continuance of the time of any fair, a Sabbath day do fall in the time of the wonted continuing of the fair, the rulers of it be commanded and authorized to stop the course of all buying and selling publicly during the time of the Sabbath day. And that all games and pastimes of shooting, bowling, cocking, bear-baiting, dancing, pieces of defence, wakes, May-games, and all other such disports, be utterly forbidden to be used

[1] *Second Part of a Register*, edit. A. Peel, p. 219.

upon any Sabbath day: and that upon great punishment to be laid upon the offenders. So that the Lord's day may be kept holy, as it is commanded." [1]

The year 1595 saw the first issue of a book which writers upon the question of Sunday usually refer to as an outstanding landmark. This was Nicholas Bound's *The True Doctrine of the Sabbath*. Fuller in his *Church History of Britain*, attributes what he terms the revival of a strict keeping of the Sunday to the publication of this book. Later writers have sometimes been content, in any reference to the history of the Protestant Sunday, to make Bound's book a starting point as if little or no attention had been paid to the subject before. It has been one of the objects of the preceding pages of this book to show that any such view of the case is incomplete and unsatisfactory. Sufficient evidence has, one hopes, been put forward to show that before 1595 the question as to the right way in which to occupy oneself upon the Sunday was one occupying many minds and one not simply for theorising about but one for practical experiment. Indeed it was the experimental part which had received perhaps the greater attention. In many cases magistrates and others were not so greatly concerned as to why people should act in such and such a way upon the Sunday as they were in seeing that their actual deeds did not interfere with the wellbeing of the participants or of others. It is, sometimes at any rate, our English way to act and then to seek for reasons which will justify our actions later. Men do not always act logically if by that phrase be meant that they have carefully thought out the reasons for their action before they performed it. Yet granted this to be so it is generally necessary sooner or later to find a reasonable ground for one's action, especially if the action is to be repeated or continued. That was the position with reference to the Sunday question when Bound's book appeared.

[1] Strype: *Annals*, Vol. III. Part 2, p. 298.

Those who were genuinely concerned about the immorality practised upon the Sunday were anxious to stop it. They traced this immorality, rightly, to the fact that people had some leisure upon the Sunday and did not know what to do with it. Many of the sports of the period, in which the people indulged in their spare time, were of a brutalizing and debasing nature such as bear-baiting. The fairs and festivities associated with the church, such as Church-ales, were often the occasion of drunkenness and loose conduct. Morally some of these sports, and of course all the excesses which might be occasioned by any of them, were wrong and ought to have been condemned altogether. Some people saw that at the time and they did condemn the practice of them upon any and every day. Such people have often been condemned and ridiculed since as narrow-minded, sour Puritans. Certainly they were mistaken in failing to differentiate between sports which had little or no justification and those which were in themselves not only harmless but healthful. But they are not the only people who failed to consider all the aspects of the case and who based their conclusions upon a partial understanding of the position. Equally myopic was the view of those who refused to see anything wrong at all in the amusements of the day and yet those people have usually escaped the censures of later generations.

There were others, and these a not negligible number, who, while not condemning honest sport and recreation, did not think it fitting that such sports should be participated in upon the Sunday. But challenged to give a reason or reasons for this belief, many of them felt at a loss. Custom and the law did not prohibit Sunday games and amusements. It was all very well to say that the day should be used for private and public devotions and for visiting the sick. Many might reply that the public services were only brief, and that therein they obtained but scanty religious instruction, so that they themselves were not equipped to spend much time in private devotions, and that their qualifications for sick-visiting were equally scanty, so that having done all that they could in this direction they still had a lot of free time. Others would point to the fact that the Court amused itself as it would upon the Sunday and that the officers of State and many private individuals worked upon the Sunday, and that therefore there was no harm in their working or playing as they chose. So those who would enforce the observance of a more devotional Sunday were in need of firmer ground upon which to base their contention.

It should never be forgotten, although very often it seems to be ignored by those who refer to the matter of Sunday amusements in Elizabeth's reign, that many, probably the majority of the people, had little or no time for sport or amusement except upon the Sunday. There was no mid-week half-holiday for shop assistants; no Saturday afternoon for the craftsman. Some sport such people might secure in the summer evenings, but probably not much. Attendance at a play would be very unlikely, because plays were always performed in the day-time then. The State had taken away many of the old holy days which, in the Middle Ages, had been in part days for recreation. So that the average Elizabethan workman was really working more days than his ancestors. But it must not be supposed that those who attacked his Sunday games were doing him necessarily a disfavour. It must be remembered that those who favoured Sunday games also thought Sunday work permissible. True, it was not to be general—but it was sufficiently countenanced to make it fairly easy for it to be undertaken in increasing measure if there ever seemed to be the need for it. If the people who desired a more devotional Sunday frowned upon Sunday games, they also would have no truck with Sunday labour.

Because Sunday was at the time the only day upon which most of the people could engage in sport and

recreation, it necessarily followed that where such pastimes led to excesses and immorality these breaches of
good-conduct took place on the Sunday. Thus, some
people condemned Sunday sports, not for any religious
motive, but simply because by prohibiting them upon
the Sunday, they would get rid of the accompanying
lawlessness. This did not mean that they condemned
sports as sports—only that they did not wish any
opportunity for large numbers of the people to be free to
amuse or indulge themselves as they liked at the same
time. It was as if to-day a person condemned Bank
holidays because of the crowds of trippers that invaded
his select beauty spot or seaside resort and made a lot
of noise and left a lot of litter, although he had no
objection at all to people taking holidays at various
times of the year, and visiting those same places then
in necessarily smaller, and therefore probably less
disconcerting, numbers. But these people were without any accepted theory upon which to base their
objection to Sunday games.

From varying motives then, but chiefly on the grounds
that Sunday games and Sunday work were not in
keeping with the devotional spirit of the day, people
had, during Elizabeth's reign, sought to restrict or
prevent Sunday labour and amusements before the
publication of Bound's book. The importance of his
book is not that it started such a movement, as has
generally been implied, but that it appeared to give a
sound, logical basis upon which to build a theory of a
stricter observation of the Sunday. In this sense it was
important.

It was Bound's book which really established the
theory that any right observation of the Sunday should
be based upon the old Mosaic law for the Sabbath. The
early Protestant writers on the subject of Sunday had,
as has been noticed, been at pains to show that the
Christian was under no necessity to observe literally the
Jewish Sabbath law. But their desires to avoid any

connection with what they regarded as Jewish superstition had led them, or some of their followers, into a rather vague position. It seems to have been a realization of the vagueness which led Bound and his supporters and disciples back to the old Jewish position.

One of the essentials of Protestantism had been from its inception the authority it placed upon the Bible. But, in the case of Luther himself, for example, it was the New Testament rather than the Old Testament which was studied and quoted at first. When Protestantism began to concern itself more with the details of moral life and conduct, then the Old Testament came to the front. This is particularly noticeable in England. It is not surprising. The world still finds the teaching of Christ, generally speaking, too baffling because to many it seems so vague or else non-existent upon so many points of moral conduct. Man still longs in times of perplexity for the 'Thou shalt' or 'Thou shalt not' however much he may gird at irksome restrictions. The Englishman, particularly, seems still to like his life to be regulated for him by positive or negative laws and by-laws even if only that he may grumble against them. So the Elizabethan moral reformer turned to the Old Testament for his support because it was so much easier to find just those clear-cut definitions there which would make his work so much plainer. Thus it was almost inevitable that when those people who sought to reform the existing condition of affairs upon the Sunday needed an authority for their claims, they should find it in the Old Testament.

Bound claimed in his book that although the Jewish ideas of priesthood, sacrifices, etc., had been taken away, the obligation of the commandment about the Sabbath remained because it was a moral commandment. The rest which that commandment ordained for the Sabbath must be a different rest from that of any other day. Scholars must not study upon that day, lawyers must not digest evidence, officers of the law must not execute warrants, there must be no recreations indulged in and men must refrain even from discussing ordinary pleasures and business. Harvest work Bound would not permit, although he would permit works of necessity with the warning "let us not imagine a necessity". He did not wish, for example, to prevent the ordinary work of cooking meals. There is the strange prohibition, found usually in the statements of those who took up a similar position to Bound, of the ringing of more than one church-bell on the Sunday. Bound seemed to have one weak point, which his enemies seized upon and that was that, while he issued a general prohibition against feasts and wedding-dinners on the Sunday, he relaxed his ban in favour of the nobility and gentlemen of quality. [1]

The position taken by Bound on the matter of Sunday amusements is worth noticing a little more in detail. He says: "Upon the Lord's Day we ought to rest from all honest recreations and lawful delights . . . because we cannot have the present delight in the use of them, and yet at the same time, be occupied in the hearing of the word, and such other parts of God's holy worship and service as he requireth of us upon the Sabbath-day." [2] This was exactly the position which others had taken up before who could not reconcile devotional exercises with ordinary pleasures. Bound himself did not condemn sports and recreations in themselves, indeed it is very important to notice that he specifies that time should be found for these upon some other day. His words are: "We do exhort them that be in government to give some time to their children and servants, for their honest recreation, upon other days, that they be not driven to take it upon this, seeing they can no more want it altogether than their ordinary food. And as we have seen that they are bound to give them some time to work for themselves, unless they will, by

[1] *Summary in Fuller's Church History*, Vol. III, pp. 158-160 and Cox: *Literature of the Sabbath Question*, Vol. I, pp. 159-160.
[2] Bound: *The True Doctrine of the Sabbath*, p. 262, quoted by Cox, p. 160.

their over-much straitness, compel them to it upon the day of rest; so must they spare also some few hours for their refreshing now and then; seeing they can no more want the one than the other."

Here then, in this book, was what many had been looking to find for some time. It was an authoritative statement based upon a Divine command. There can be no doubt that many accepted the teaching of the book gladly. Fuller, writing some sixty years later, gives, no doubt, a somewhat exaggerated statement of the influence of the book, but it is worth recording what he says. His conclusion is: "It is almost incredible how taking this doctrine was, partly because of its purity, and partly for the eminent piety of such persons as maintained it; so that the Lord's Day, especially in corporations, began to be precisely kept, people became a law to themselves, forbearing such sports as yet by statute permitted, yea, many rejoiced at their own restraint therein. On this day the stoutest fencer laid down the buckler—the most skilful archer unbent his bow, counting all shooting beside the mark; May-games and morris-dances grew out of request: and good reason that bells should be silenced from jingling about men's legs if their very ringing in steeples was adjudged unlawful. Some of them were ashamed of their former pleasures, like children, which, grown bigger, blush themselves out of their rattles and whistles. Others forbore them for fear of their superiors; and many left them out of a politic compliance, lest otherwise they should be accounted licentious". [1]

Such an ideal state of affairs as was pictured by Fuller was certainly not widespread in the country at the end of Elizabeth's reign, as we have seen. Had it been it might have been better for the future history of the people generally, for on the whole Bound's position is the position which the country eventually came to adopt on the matter of Sunday observance. Probably

[1] Fuller: *Church History*, Vol. III, p. 159.

the chief result of Bound's book was to focus attention upon the question of Sunday observance to a much greater degree and crystallize the thought of those who had been for long dissatisfied with the existing state of the country. If it achieved successes for the supporters of a more devout use of the Sunday, it also roused those who desired no change. Having quoted Fuller's glowing account of the support which the book won, it will be well to set over against that Fuller's account of the criticisms levelled at the book. In this connection Fuller says: "Yet learned men were much divided in their judgments about these Sabbatarian doctrines. Some embraced them as ancient truths consonant to Scripture, long disused and neglected, now seasonably revived for the increasing of piety. Others conceived them grounded on a wrong bottom; but because they tended to the manifest advance of religion, it was a pity to oppose them, seeing none have just reason to complain, being deceived in their own good. But a third sort flatly fell out with these positions as galling men's necks with a Jewish yoke against the liberty of Christians; that Christ, as Lord of the Sabbath, had removed the rigour thereof; and allowed men lawful recreations: that this doctrine put an unequal lustre on the Sunday on set purpose to eclipse all other holy days, to the derogation of the authority of the church; that this strict observance was set up out of faction to be a character of difference, to brand all for libertines who did not entertain it".[1]

The last point that Fuller makes here is one that deserves particular attention. Bound's book was distasteful to those in high authority in State and Church. That is understandable, because it advocated changes which they themselves had been desired to make in the direction of a stricter control of people's habits upon the Sunday and which they had refused to make, as we have seen. The doctrine upon which the claim for a

[1] Fuller, Vol. III, p. 160.

stricter Sunday was based was not the official doctrine of the State Church. It was not a day when anyone even dreamed of toleration in religious matters, and therefore this new presentment in a visible form of a feeling which had been slowly taking shape for some time must be annihilated. Whitgift as Archbishop of Canterbury, and Popham, the Lord Chief Justice, as representing the forces of the Church and the State therefore tried to suppress the book, with the usual result that they increased the demand for it and probably increased the number of those who supported the views it voiced.

It is also understandable that those who opposed the ideas of the book should claim, as some of them seem to have done, that those who supported these ideas did so, not because they really believed in them, but because by so doing they could attack the existing Church system. That is to say, the moral reformers, or Puritans in the sense of those who desired a greater purity of morals, were lumped together with the anti-Anglican Puritans, or those who desired to change the established form of religion and the whole collection was charged with using the idea of a need for Sabbatarianism as a weapon for attacking the authority of Anglicanism. This was a charge which was to be repeatedly made before the controversy over the Sunday question had ceased to be a keen one. But while from the point of view of fighting tactics at the time we can appreciate, while not applauding, this stroke, it is not nearly so understandable that historians of a later date should accept this theory. For example Jeremy Collier in his *Ecclesiastical History of Great Britain*, published in 1714, wrote concerning the publication of Bound's book: "The Puritans having miscarried in their open attacks upon the Church, endeavoured to carry on their designs more under covert. Their magnifying the Sabbath-Day, as they call Sunday, was a serviceable expedient for this purpose". [1]

[1] J. Collier: *An Ecclesiastical History of Great Britain*, Vol. II, p. 643.

There seems to be no evidence to support such a view as Collier expresses. As we have seen, many of those who supported the position to which Bound's book had given authoritative expression were of the moral-Puritan type. That is to say, they were in very many cases within the Anglican Church, and they had no desire to change the constitution of that Church, but only to improve the moral state of the country. That there was a need for such an improvement, particularly in regard to the observation of Sunday, there is plenty of evidence to prove. With regard to the anti-Anglican Puritans, there is nothing to prove that they in any way exaggerated the position with regard to the Sunday in order to secure their object of overthrowing the existing State Church. Naturally the fact that the State Church condoned officially what they considered to be a lax and irreligious state of affairs would be yet another strong argument for the overthrow of that State Church as it then existed. But to say that they put forward this argument simply because they wanted to overthrow the Church is to put the cart before the horse.

It seems likely that the fact that there were those who were known to be opposed to the Anglican system amongst those who, on purely moral grounds, supported a stricter Sunday did harm to the cause. The main issue, the need for a more devotional Sunday, tended to be obscured in the struggle over the Establishment. Those who advocated a Sunday free from work and amusements and devoted wholly to religious observances were all branded as Puritans, by which term was meant enemies of Anglicanism. As a consequence many of the friends of a reformed Sunday within the ranks of the Anglican church were reduced to silence or misrepresented. So effectively was this done that it is still the popular idea that the only people who wanted to restrict Sunday games—the matter of Sunday work is usually ignored—were the Puritans, meaning thereby

5

those who dissented from the Anglican system and whose outlook on life was narrow and gloomy.

So much space has been given to a consideration of the influence of Bound's book because the book was a focus point at which were concentrated tendencies which had been developing for many years and from which started a very keen controversy. Here then this chapter can conveniently end with the addition only of two brief quotations expressing the thoughts of individuals upon the matter of Sunday observance after the date of Bound's work. The first is in a letter dated February 18th, 1599, from Sir Edward Coke to Sir Robert Cecil and shows that the question of the lawfulness or otherwise of Sunday work was certainly one which occupied the minds of people even though they might not subscribe to the theory that to work on the Sunday was wrong. Coke says, after referring to work which he has done "to perfect four commissions" that: "If I were not persuaded *Quod bonum est bene-facere in Sabbate,* I should think that I had broken the whole Sabbath yesterday in speeding of this business, and now do mean in satisfaction of nature's due to shrove on my bed". [1] The other is a quotation which appears in the diary of a member of the Middle Temple, John Manningham, written in January, 1602. "The spending of the afternoons on Sundays, either idly or about temporal affairs, is like dipping the Queen's coin; this treason to the Prince, that profanation, and robbing God of his own". [2]

People at the end of Elizabeth's reign did not accept as lightly as they had done at the beginning the idea that once the religious duties of the day, as prescribed by the Church, were over, they could do just as they liked on Sunday.

---

[1] *Calendar of Manuscripts of the Marquis of Salisbury,* Vol. VII, p. 74.
[2] *Diary of John Manningham,* edit. J. Bruce, p. 15.

CHAPTER VI

THE SITUATION IN THE REIGN OF JAMES I UP TO THE ISSUE OF THE DECLARATION OF SPORTS IN 1618

THE Puritan party within the State Church, that is, those who desired a greater latitude in the matter of ritual and those who desired a greater degree of moral reform, hoped at the beginning of James I's reign that he would be sympathetic to their claims. One of the points put forward in their Millenary Petition, which led to the calling of the Hampton Court Conference in 1604, was a request that "the Lord's day may not be profaned, nor the observation of other holidays strictly enjoined".[1] The latter demand had become coupled with the former in Puritan minds for several reasons. One was the fact that they thought the observation of too many Church festivals was a waste of time. Another objection which they had to them was that they were relics of Roman Catholicism and therefore to be swept aside. Thirdly, and this was with many a particularly vital point, they thought that for any other days to be classed as equal with the Sunday was to detract from the value and sacredness of the Sunday. As we have seen, they claimed to find divine command for the observance of Sunday in the Bible: they certainly could not find any such command for the keeping of Saints' days and other Church festivals. They wished all that was done to be based upon the authority of the Bible, not merely upon some State decree.

In the Hampton Court Conference reference was made to the profanation of the Sunday, and general

[1] Gee and Hardy: *Documents illustrative of English Church History*, p. 509.

assent seems to have been given to stricter measures for reform of existing abuses being taken. In the Convocation which followed, Elizabeth's Injunctions with reference to the observance of Sunday were revived and incorporated in Canon 13 which said: "All manner of persons within the Church of England shall from henceforth celebrate and keep the Lord's day, commonly called Sunday, and other holy days, according to God's holy will and pleasure, and the orders of the Church of England prescribed in that behalf, viz., in hearing the word of God read and taught, in private and public prayers, in acknowledging their offences to God, and amendment of the same, in reconciling themselves charitably to their neighbours, where ill pleasure has been, in oftentimes receiving the communion of the Body and Blood of Christ, using all godly and sober conversation". [1] Heylyn, the champion of the Anglican position on the question of Sunday observance in the next reign considered this Canon an excellent piece of work because it stopped the profaneness of which complaint had been made and because it continued to rank the holy days with the Sunday, and he seems surprised that the Puritans were not satisfied. [2] Perhaps we may venture to a greater sympathy with the Puritan position. As we have just seen, they objected strongly to any equality of standing between the Sunday and any other days and therefore could hardly be expected to accept that interpretation of the Canon. Thus, although Heylyn may have felt satisfied theoretically that the Canon prevented all profaneness, the Puritans, more in touch with the realities of the situation, knew very well it would not so act. It did not mention Sunday sports and recreations and therefore the people who desired those things would undoubtedly take it that those amusements were permissible. This, in itself would, as we have seen, be against the convictions of

---

[1] *History of the Sabbath*, P. Heylyn, Book II, p. 258, also Walcott: *Constitutions and Canons of the Church of England*, p. 19.
[2] Heylyn, ditto.

many, if not all, of the Puritans, and apart from this they, and many others, would know only too well that if sports and recreations were permitted they would in themselves lead in many cases to conduct which could be no other than profanation of the Sunday.

Of much more value from the Puritan point of view and much more important in the struggle which was being carried on to improve the amenities of the Sunday, was the reference to Sunday made in the royal proc- lamation of the previous year. In this proclamation, issued on the 7th of May, 1603, it was stated: "For that we are informed that there hath been heretofore great neglect in this Kingdom of keeping the Sabbath-day, for better observing of the same, and avoiding of all impious profanation of it, we do straitly charge and command that no bear-baiting, bull-baiting, interludes, common plays, or other like disordered and unlawful exercises and pastimes, be frequented, kept, or used at any time hereafter upon the sabbath-day." [1] This is a significant statement for it shows that the optimistic picture of the reform secured by the popularity of Bound's book was not as widespread as might be expected from Fuller's reference to it. It shows too that those in authority were aware of the fact that all was not well in the conduct of many upon the Sunday, or James, who must presumably have acted upon the advice or with the concurrence of those at the Court who knew more of the state of affairs than he could possibly do, would not have referred to the matter so early in his reign.

This proclamation would not do all that the Puritans desired, hence presumably their efforts in the Hampton Court Conference. Ordinary Sunday games were still permissible. It was the more brutalizing exhibitions calculated to gather together the rougher elements of the people or to bring out the worst features of those

[1] Quoted Strype: *Annals*, Vol. IV, p. 531. *Tudor and Stuart Proclamations*, edit. R. Steele No. 944.

who had assembled that were forbidden. Plays too, which even Elizabeth had felt it necessary to ban within the City of London, were probably forbidden not so much for themselves as for the opportunity which they seem to have afforded for loose conduct amongst those who assembled to witness them. But that such things were declared illegal upon the Sunday was a sign that those who had agitated for such reforms in the previous reign had not been unreasonable in their demands and that the officials of the State themselves were coming to see that the policy of letting people spend much of the Sunday just as they pleased was not satisfactory.

In the light of this proclamation it seems reasonable to suppose that some more definite statement about Sunday recreations might have appeared in the Thirteenth Canon which resulted from the Hampton Court Conference but for the fact that the result of that conference was to refuse any measure of comprehension to the Puritan party. The idea of a stricter control over people's conduct upon the Sunday was by now irrevocably linked with the Puritan party and now that the ban of excommunication had gone out against all who would not subscribe in detail to the Anglican position it was unlikely that the Anglican party would of themselves advocate what was regarded as a Puritan doctrine. Too much, on the other hand, must not be read into the Proclamation. There is no evidence that James I was personally any more anxious to curtail the liberty of people to do as they liked upon the Sunday than Elizabeth had been. He himself certainly possessed no strict theories on the matter. The meetings of the Council seem to have continued upon the Sunday just as they had done in Elizabeth's reign and the King and his Court enjoyed themselves upon that day much as they pleased. For example, we read in January, 1608, of a masque being performed at the Court on a Sunday evening,[1] and other incidents which point to the hold-

[1] J. Nichols: *Progresses of King James I*, Vol. II. p. 163.

ing by the King of a very broad theory as to Sunday pleasures will be noticed later.

Now that there was a much more definite breach between Anglican and Puritan the controversy over the right theory about the Sunday and the right practice upon that day grew more intense. In 1606 Bound's book was re-issued as a clear and challenging statement of the Puritan position. It was answered by Thomas Rogers, chaplain to Archbishop Bancroft, in his book, *The Catholic Doctrine of the Church of England*, published in 1607. Drafts of the book had appeared earlier but it was in its full form as it appeared in 1607 that it strove to combat the Puritan theory of the Sunday. One paragraph from Rogers' book is worth quoting as showing, allowing of course for the exaggerated language of controversial writing, how in some places the stricter theory of Sunday observance has been carried to extreme lengths. Unfortunately since, as then, those who made the wildest statements were too frequently taken as typical instead of being treated as exceptional.

Rogers says: "I have read (and many there be alive which will justify it) how it was preached in a market-town in Oxfordshire, that to do any servile work or business on the Lord's Day is as great a sin as to kill a man, or to commit adultery. It was preached in Somersetshire that to throw a bowl on the Sabbath-day is as great a sin as to kill a man. It was preached in Norfolk, that to make a feast or wedding-dinner on the Lord's day is as great a sin as for a father to take a knife and cut his child's throat. It was preached in Suffolk (I can name the man, and I was present when he was convented before his ordinary for preaching the same) that to ring more bells than one upon the Lord's day to call the people unto the Church is as great a sin as to commit murder." [1]

When one realizes that the Puritans had been driven

[1] T. Rogers: *The Catholic Doctrine of the Church of England*, edit. J. J. S. Perowne, p. 19.

to base their arguments for a stricter Sunday upon the
Fourth Commandment and when one realizes, too, the
authority which the Bible, particularly the Old Testament, had for them it is perhaps not as shocking as it
seems at first reading to find such views expressed.
After all there was nothing in the Mosaic code to suggest
that one commandment was of greater importance than
another and therefore the idea that to break one was as
serious as to break another was very easy of attainment. Then, too, as we have seen, the Puritans saw
that only very drastic measures could win many of the
people from their allegiance to Sunday jollification.
The Puritans are by no means the only group of people
to have used anathemas to attempt to enforce their
particular ideas upon a heedless or hostile public
although they seem to have met with an undue share of
censure from Posterity for so doing.

Rogers himself in his book expressed the orthodox
Anglican view of the time. He took the chief points of
the Puritan position and denied the validity of them.
As he expressed it: "They are greatly deceived which
think that:—it is not lawful for us to use the seventh
day to any other end, but to the holy and sanctified end
for which God in the beginning created it: all the
Judicial days and feasts being taken away, only the
Sabbath remaineth: we are bound unto the same rest
with the Jews on the Sabbath day: we be restrained
upon the Sabbath from work, both hand and foot, as the
Jews were: every ecclesiastical minister in his charge
necessarily must preach and make a sermon every
Sabbath-day; every man or woman, under pain of utter
condemnation, must hear a sermon every Sunday."[1]

What appears to be a very moderate and sane
treatise putting the point of view of the advocates of a
stricter Sunday than Rogers desired appeared about
this time. It was written by Richard Greenham and in

---

[1] T. Rogers: *The Catholic Doctrine of the Church of England*, edit. J. J. S. Perowne,
p. 315.

it he objected to any work upon the Sunday except such labour as could not be carried out on the previous day or left until the Monday. But "milking of kine, making of beds, and dressing of meats, as for travellers, bakers and brewers, that their business, if it be necessary, must be done either early in the morning or later in the evening."[1] Ordinary travelling he would not allow but he made an exception in the case of physicians and lawyers—why the latter it is not at all clear. It cannot be too often emphasized that this objection to Sunday work was a very important social contribution which was made by the supporters of a stricter Sunday. Greenham of course would not permit Sunday amusements.

It will be well now to consider, as far as it is possible to obtain information, what the actual state of affairs in the country was like up to the time when attention was once more directed to the question of Sunday observance by the action of James I in issuing his "Declaration concerning Lawful Sports" in 1618. The Royal proclamation forbidding bear-baiting seems to have been a dead letter if we can accept a statement made, presumably by a man plying with a vehicle for public hire, in 1604, which runs as follows: "I waited for another fare, but then I bethought myself again that all the fares went by water—on Sundays—to the bear-baiting."[2]

That the law even as it stood, that is to say, permitting many games provided they were not played until after the hours of Divine Worship, was often broken there seems to be every indication. Here again there was much to strengthen the position taken up by the advocates of a stricter Sunday. The freedom granted to the people to play upon the Sunday once their devotional duties were over was abused, and the Sunday thereby still more profaned. For example, the York-

[1] Richard Greenham: *A Treatise of the Sabbath*, edit. of 1612, p. 164.
[2] Quoted in Govett: *King's Book of Sports*, p. 67.

shire justices in 1606 at Malton dealt with several cases
of this sort. The records of the quarter sessions tell us
of the trial of "Walter Parkhurst, of Sheriff Hutton,
victualler or alehousekeeper, for receiving into his house
during the time of Divine service on Sundays and holy
days, and other days, and suffering him to remain there
for more than one hour, one Tho. Wildon, a person
excommunicated for not coming to church for two or
three years last past, and lodging him, especially of late,
and also for receiving his brother, Fr. Wildon, at like
times, who is not seen to come to church; and also for
keeping guile-bones or Ten Bones and other unlawful
games at his house, for men's servants and apprentices
to play in the time of evening prayer of the Sabbath
days and other days".[1] The same sessions saw the
case of Cuthbert Cowston of Normanby who "admitted
to keep an alehouse there, for making on two several
Sabbath days in June last drinkings or garries whereby
above the number of a hundred persons were assembled
together with pipes and drums and dancing all the time
of Divine service, in the afternoons of the said Sabbath
days, contrary to the condition of his recognizance for
alehousekeeping".[2]

The reference to the drinking in times of service being
contrary to the alehousekeepers' recognizance reminds
us that all alehousekeepers had to obtain a licence from
the local justices in those days before they could do
business. This licence always contained some provision
of the nature indicated in the last extract. For example,
we have a copy of a licence issued by the Norfolk
magistrates in 1608 which contained eight conditions,
the third of which was: "That you suffer none to tipple
in your house upon Sabbath or festival days in the time
of the sermon or divine services, nor at any time after
nine of the clock at night".[3]

[1] *Quarter Sessions Records of the North Riding of Yorkshire*, edit. J. C. Atkinson,
Vol. I, p. 49.
[2] Ditto, p. 50.
[3] *Official Papers of Sir N. Bacon*, edit. H. W. Saunders, pp. 34 5.

In 1613 the Yorkshire magistrates had to deal with "Robert Kendrawe of Osmotherley for using bowling on the Sabbath days in the church-yard in the time of Divine Service; and also Tho. Lowicke, gentleman and Rob. Ingeram of the same, for the like".[1] There certainly seemed a need for some stricter rule for the Sunday if only on the grounds of decency when such a state of affairs as bowling in the church-yard while service went on within the church was possible. That such a thing was done, although not lawful and therefore, as we have just seen, punishable, shows that what people needed was not a mere tightening up of the law, but a more positive teaching with regard to the meaning of the Sunday, which the existing doctrines of the Anglican church did not supply. Therein was an excuse, if not a justification, for the extreme and falsely-grounded Puritan teaching.

Two years later the Yorkshire justices were faced with a similar state of affairs when they dealt with "Two Forcell men as usual profaners of the Sabbath day by bowling all the afternoon till night, and did not repair to the church to Evening Prayer".[2] Other instances of the punishment of people by the Yorkshire justices for playing games upon the Sunday or for drinking during the hours of service can be found in the county records.

Turning to another part of the country, we find amongst the presentments before the justices at Wells in Somersetshire in 1610 the following entry: "John Antonie the younger, Henry Antonie, William Pontet, and Robert Tauntone, at Wells aforesaid, played at unlawful games, to wit, bowls in time of divine service against the form of the Statute".[3] This entry is in Latin and the translator of it for the report of the Historical Manuscripts Commission questions the meaning of the original Latin word "globus" which may

---

[1] *Quarter Sessions Records*, Vol. II, p. 34.
[2] Ditto, p. 108.
[3] *Historical Manuscripts Commission*, 15th Report, p. 350.

mean bowls or marbles. Bowls seems the more probable translation! In any case the implication is the same— that the Sunday was not properly observed. Bowling for the ordinary people had been made unlawful at any time by an Act of Henry VIII [1] so that the reference here may be to the illegality of the men's playing bowls at all, or more likely to the illegality of their playing during the time of Divine Worship.

The Justices in Devonshire seem to have been concerned to suppress the holding of Church-ales and other festivities of a like nature upon the Sunday, although as far as the policy of the State with regard to Sunday was concerned such things were quite lawful. It was the drunkenness and loose conduct attendant upon such celebrations that determined the magistrates in their policy. An order of the Justices in 1607 suppressed all Church-ales, clerk's ales and all similar revels. [2] Evidently the order was not enforced properly, or was not authoritative enough, for on July 24th, 1615, the Assize Court at Exeter took the matter up. Its order said: "The several manslaughters committed at two Church-ales within the county since the beginning of this present month of July, and further advertisements given unto this Court of the continual profanation of God's Sabbath at these and other such like unlawful meetings, ministers unto the court just occasion to recite an order formerly set down by the reverend judge of assize at the assizes holden for this county, the 19th day of July in the year of the reign of our sovereign Lord King James . . . the 11th . . . that order being as follows viz:— It is ordered by the Court in regard of the infinite number of inconveniences daily arising by means of revels, Church-ales, and bull-baitings, that all such revels, Church-ales, and bull-baitings be from henceforth utterly suppressed". [3]

It will be seen by the order that the judge and the

[1] 33 Henry VIII, Cap. ix.
[2] *Quarter Sessions from Elizabeth to Anne*, edit. A. H. A. Hamilton, p. 73.
[3] Quoted by Prynne: *Canterburies Doome*, p. 153.

magistrates refer specifically to the profanation of the Sunday. Theirs is not the heated language of the fanatic any more than it is his warped view, but a sober recognition by those accustomed to view things calmly that people were not spending the Sunday as they ought. They too refer to bull-baitings: evidently such things still continued in spite of the royal proclamation against them. All points to the fact that it was a very difficult task to change the habits of the people, particularly those habits which were conducive to the greatest amount of lawless behaviour.

One may only speculate as to whether there was any necessary connection between the state of affairs just described and an order made some six months previously to the clergy of the diocese of Exeter. This order is reported as follows in the diary of Walter Yonge, who was a Justice of the Peace and a member of parliament for Honiton: "16th Dec. 1614. This day the ministers of this diocese were called before the Bishop of Exon, who read letters from the Archbishop, the effect of which were that every minister should exhort his parishioners to continue together the Sabbath day, and not to wander to other preachers who have better gifts than their own pastors, but should content themselves with the word of God read, and Homilies". [1] A diet of reading and homilies would be hardly strong enough meat to tempt those who had been long accustomed to the delights of a careless Sunday to a more sober and profitable spending of the day. Some more definite and authoritative religious instruction was going to be needed to achieve any great change. It might be well to discourage the people from wandering about as idle "sermon-tasters". But steps ought to have been taken to provide each parish with a minister capable of teaching his people himself without falling back upon the lazy device of reading a homily.

[1] *Diary of Walter Yonge*, edit. G. Roberts, p. 24.

Other parts of the country afford evidence that the local authorities, as in the reign of Elizabeth, were more zealous to act in defence of a soberer and more restful Sunday than the central authorities of State or Church. In the records of Shewsbury, probably for 1605, we read: "Petition to the bailiffs from William Gylson, milner, imprisoned for profaning the Sabbath day, in carrying of meal and travelling with his ware, contrary to their proclamation".[1] Evidently the by-laws in Shrewsbury were stricter than the national laws and this before the Puritans are usually considered to have influenced, directly at any rate, State or local policy. There is an undated memorandum in the records of Canterbury which is placed as belonging to the early seventeenth century to the effect that four men were "admonished for taking bread on Sundays and holidays".[2] In 1611 at Salisbury the Wardens of the Taylors' Company were imprisoned for patronizing morris-dancers on the Sunday and were only allowed bail after they had been admonished by the mayor for profaning the Sunday.[3]

The Middlesex Justices in 1614 issued an order against butchers and others doing general trading upon the Sunday, and they justify their order by saying that "great abuse is committed within the parts adjacent to the City of London in this County of Middlesex by poulterers, butchers and other persons that do keep open shambles and sell their wares and commodities upon the Sabbath day to the great dishonour of Almighty God and the slander of religion and government".[4]

An interesting side-light upon the effect of the growing disposition to treat the Sunday as a day free from all unnecessary labour is contained in the account of a controversy that arose about this subject between a

---

[1] *Historical Manuscripts Commission*, Fifteenth Report, p. 63.
[2] *Historical Manuscripts Commission*, Vol. I for 1901, p. 231.
[3] *Calendar State Papers Domestic, James I*, Vol. LXIV, p. 50.
[4] Jeaffreson: *Middlesex County Records*, Vol. II, p. 107.

professor in Gresham College, London, and a Chester minister. Edward Brerewood, the professor, had a nephew who was apprenticed in London. Recently the nephew's master had sent him to Chester on business and in Chester the apprentice had come under the influence of Mr. Nicholas Byfield, a minister who evidently held strict views about Sunday observance. A change had taken place in the attitude of the apprentice to Sunday work as a result, a change with which the uncle does not agree. The uncle found his nephew in a worried state of mind, the reason for which Mr. Brerewood describes as follows: "His master on the Lord's day sent him forth sometimes on errands, as to bid guests, or fetch wine, or give his horse provender (which last his master remembereth not that ever he bade him past once) or about some other light business: and he was instructed (he said) to do these things or any other work on the Sabbath day, although it were such work as might lawfully be done on another day, and although he did it not of his own disposition, but only in obedience to his master's command, yet was a sin." [1]

This incident took place in 1611 and shows that the idea of preventing Sunday labour was becoming more prominent. Perhaps the attitude taken up by Mr. Byfield, who defends his position in a reply to Mr. Brerewood, will be more understandable when we remember the prevailing official attitude towards the keeping of Sunday. It may seem quibbling over trifles to-day to object to the carrying out of such light duties as are mentioned in the case in point. But if these were allowed where was the dividing line to be drawn? Such a position may be termed, as it so often is, narrow, or fanatic, or ridiculous, but it was a position which was to have very valuable results for the nation. In opposition to it was set out a doctrine which had in it the seeds of untold controversy and potential abuse. This doctrine is voiced by Mr. Brerewood when he argues

[1] *A Learned Treatise of the Sabbath* by Edward Brerewood, p. 3.

that the fourth commandment applies only to masters
and not to servants. He concludes, therefore, that
servants must work if the master command them
"because God hath no way forbidden them that; God
hath indeed forbidden the masters *exacting* that work
on the *Sabbath*; but he hath not forbidden the servants
execution of that work if it be demanded or exacted . . .
for although I acknowledge the servant's work on
the Sabbath to imply sin; yet I say it is not the
servant's fault".[1]

Such a line of thought was capable of far-reaching
extension. Presumably, following such reasoning, it
would be possible for the authorities in State or State
Church to command the people to work in the ordinary
way on the Sunday, and although the people might
regard such a command as sinful they would be bound
to obey it as the servants of the State. There would be
no room for any development of democratic ideas in
such a theory. Without taking the principle to that extreme, and probably Brerewood never saw the possibility of that deduction although there were those in
the State who would not have been unwilling to have
made it, we may fairly speculate on the use which un-
scrupulous masters would have made of it, if not in the
seventeenth century, certainly at the end of the
eighteenth. Socially as well as politically those who
stood for the right of the individual to freedom from
work on the Sunday did a great service not only to their
own generation but to all succeeding generations. It
might be, indeed it was actually so, that in the struggle
to obtain to right of freedom from work what appeared
to be the old freedom to play was to a great extent, if not
entirely, lost. But, as we shall see, the result, socially
and without any regard for the religious point of view,
was worth that loss which in itself was to be more than
compensated for later by Saturday and mid-week
holidays and half-holidays. Also the more the position

---

[1] *A Learned Treatise of the Sabbath* by Edward Brerewood, p. 27.

is studied the clearer it seems to be that, without the loss, there could not have been the gain. The demand for a Sunday free from work had to be based on the fourth commandment, and the taking up of that position, as we have shown, implied the abstention from Sunday sports.

The tendency to restrict the freedom of the people to indulge in Sunday sports because that freedom so often degenerated into licence was increasing, as has been noticed. A further illustration of this fact may be found in certain happenings in Worcestershire. In 1617 a certain William Jefferies petitioned the Justices of the Peace for Worcestershire to enforce a stricter observance of the Sunday, and in his petition he instances several occasions in past years upon which the day has been profaned. He shows that it has been customary for the people of Longdon every year to indulge in May-games, dancing and sports on the Sunday with the result that people have come to Longdon from other places to join in these amusements, and a lot of ruffianism and drunkenness has resulted therefrom. In 1614 for example a number of men from Fortington visited the sports and a riot ensued and one man got a broken head. In 1615 men from Elsfield caused a riot which ended in some of the offenders having to appear before the magistrates. It was not only the outsiders who were blameworthy however for, also in 1615, when the Sunday sports were stopped at the time of evening service, on one occasion some of the young people of Longdon forced an excommunicated woman into the church during the time of the service and sent a boy in with her to call out and proclaim her presence, hoping thus to stop the service and so be free to continue their sports. In the following year Jefferies, who was then the constable for Longdon, tried to arrest the musician who was playing for the Sunday dancing in order to punish him under the law against rogues, but had to desist under threats of

6

violence. So these sports and dancings still continue in 1617, and because of the quarrelling and disorder which is likely to be repeated Jefferies petitions for their suppression. The Justices ordered the prosecution of those who profaned the Sunday by dancing or playing during Divine Service, or who caused any riot or disturbance.[1]

It was incidents like these, and no doubt, had we the complete records, they could be paralleled from the happenings of every county, that swelled the ranks of those who sought to curtail all amusements upon the Sunday and, indeed, justified their objective. People were not content to restrict their games and amusements either within the bounds of decency or within the times permitted. Those who played upon the Sunday, like the youth of Longdon, did not see why their play should cease when the time for service came. This in itself is not very surprising. As the people who urged a stricter keeping of the Sunday—the Puritans both within and without the Anglican Church—saw, it would only be by making Sunday a day apart from the other days, a day when neither work nor sport was permissible, that people would come to realize the sacredness of the day. On the other hand, the King and his advisers seem either to have been blind to the abuses so often committed on the Sunday, or else to have thought that these abuses could be dealt with by the existing laws without in any way curtailing the liberty of the subject to amuse himself as he wished, provided he kept the law and attended church. At any rate nothing was done officially to remedy these abuses, and indeed James I was soon to surprise many in the country by definitely giving his support to the idea of continuing the old established custom of Sunday amusements. The events leading up to the royal Book of Sports were entirely local in character and took place in the County of Lancashire, and a consideration of these events will be best left to the next chapter.

[1] Records of Worcester: *Historical Manuscripts Report for* 1901, Vol. 1.

CHAPTER VII

THE DECLARATION OF SPORTS AND EVENTS CONNECTED THEREWITH

REFERENCE has been made in Chapter IV to the determined attempts that had been made in certain parts of Lancashire in the latter part of Elizabeth's reign to remedy the abuses connected with the observation of the Sunday. That those abuses had not ceased and that the determination on the part of some, at any rate, of the local authorities to suppress them had not waned will be seen when the state of affairs existing in the following reign is considered. It is worth while and indeed imperative to do this because writers who deal with the subject of James I's Declaration of Sports have, in the past, failed to take sufficient, or in many cases any, notice of the condition of affairs in Lancashire before James I saw fit to interfere. This has resulted in the mistaken notion that James's Declaration was the one authoritative statement issued to combat the meddling of a number of Puritan busybodies who entirely misrepresented the wishes of the bulk of the people and whose actions had no support from responsible quarters. The facts point to something somewhat different.

In the first year of the reign of James I there is the record of the presentment before the magistrates at Preston of James Sturyaker and some forty others "on 26th June last, being Sunday, . . . assembled at Garstang and played a drum and fife and with branches rode and walked from a certain wood as far as Kirkeland in Garstang." [1] In the following year at Manchester

[1] *Lancashire Quarter Sessions Records*, edit. J. Tait, Vol. I, p. 173.

a man called Digle was forbidden by the magistrates
to keep an alehouse because of evidence that he "doth
most usually keep drinking and tipling in his house
upon the Sabbath day in the afternoon in the time of
divine service." [1]

A connection between the profanation of the Sunday
and the holding of Roman Catholic views, to which
earlier reference has been made, was one which some,
at any rate, still believed to exist. Thus a certain John
Wryht could send to his friend Edmond Hopwood in
1609 with reference to their proposed meeting with
each other at Standish when "we shall have time to
confer . . . of the ruins of the church of God (in) many
places of the county, by reason of the increase of
Papistes' profaning of the Sabbath and other enormities which the most are not ashamed to commit
without remorse of conscience or fear of the law." [2]

In 1616 the Justices of the Peace for Lancashire
issued with the approval of the Judge of Assize certain
orders with reference to the keeping of the Sunday
which are very useful in furnishing evidence of what
the local authorities of that county thought of the
existing state of affairs and of the way existing abuses
needed remedying. These orders are as follows:— [3]

"1. First that there be no wares or victuals sold or
shewed upon any Sunday (necessary victuals only
excepted) and that no butcher sell any flesh upon
any Sunday after the second peal ended to morning
prayer nor yet at any time in the afternoon upon the
Sabbath day and that every person so offending
presently be brought by the Constable before some
justice of the peace to be bound by him to the good
behaviour and to appear at the next assize after he
is so bound.
2. That no Householder after the beginning of the

[1] *Lancashire Quarter Sessions Records*, edit. J. Tait, Vol. I, p. 216.
[2] *Historical Manuscripts Report of the MSS. of Lord Kenyon*, p. 16.
[3] *Manchester Sessions*, edit. E. Axon, Vol. I, pp. 15-17.

last peal to morning prayer suffer any person (not being of the household) to eat, drink, or remain in their house in time of Divine service but shall shut their doors up to the end that all persons within the said house may go to the church: if any be found in any alehouse in time of Divine service the said alehouse to be put down and henceforth not to be licensed again."

The third order compelled every alehousekeeper to submit to the inspection of his house by the rightful authorities to see that good order was kept. The fourth order said that: "Every alehousekeeper with his wife and family shall come to the church every Sunday as well upon pain to lose and forfeit 12d. as to be discharged from brewing except they shall have a lawful and reasonable excuse to the contrary." The fifth order said that: "such persons as shall be found walking, talking or idle, standing either in the church-yard or market place in time of Divine service shall pay 12d. a piece and are to be bound to the good behaviour and to appear at the next assizes."

It may be said that so far these orders go no further than the accepted policy of the State and the State Church at the time. That is so but it is surely significant that the magistrates found it necessary in that case to issue these orders at all at such a date. Evidently the actual practice of many of the people did not conform even with the minimum requirements of the law. Had it been possible to get *all* the people into the regular habit of attending Divine Worship twice upon the Sunday and had it been possible to provide them in that worship with real spiritual instruction and comfort, then probably there would have been little need to attempt to legislate as to what all these people should or should not do for the remainder of the day. But it was not possible to get them all to attend church, and those who did were in many cases not edified by the

service and consequently not only did they cause
annoyance to the devoutly minded during the time of
the day when, according to the theory of the Church,
they should have been engaged in private meditation
or sick-visiting, but also during those times when the
law of the land said they ought to be attending public
devotions.

But the orders of the Lancashire justices did not
stop at a mere attempt to re-inforce existing State
legislation. After the sixth order, which provided for
the punishment of such constables and churchwardens
as refused to enforce these commands, came the
seventh which said: "That there be no piping, dancing
(bowling, bear or bull-baiting) or any other profanation
upon any Sabbath day in any part of the day: or upon
any festival day in time of Divine service." Above the
words in brackets was written "unlawful" signifying
as was of course the case, that bowling, bear and bull-
baiting upon the Sunday were not permitted by the
State and implying, as of course was also the case, that
in prohibiting other things the magistrates were acting
upon their own authority and were in advance of the
State. It is quite clear that the magistrates of Lancashire, supported by the Judge of Assize, were determined to enforce a much stricter observance of the
Sunday than was common at the time. Evidently,
although they do not expressly mention all sports in
their order, they meant to put an end to all Sunday
amusements for, after the publication of the King's
declaration, which expressly allowed certain Sunday
games, there was written beside the seventh order the
statement: "piping, dancing, vaulting, leaping, shooting
etc. lawful upon Sundays by the King's Declaration."
Clearly therefore the magistrates had originally meant
to ban all these and only qualified their rule at a later
date because it clashed with the royal command.

Of course not all the gentlemen of Lancashire, let
alone the ordinary folk, would agree with the ideas of

the magistrates. Possibly left to themselves the individual magistrates in their private capacity would not have desired to keep such a strict Sunday. The point is that in their official capacity, as guardians of the peace and well-being of the county, they felt it necessary to restrict the freedom of the people to do just as they liked. Their action in most cases was prompted by their consideration of what was expedient rather than by any Puritan theories of the sacredness of the Sunday.

We have preserved for us in the journal of a certain Nicholas Assheton of Downham, in Lancashire, which he kept during part of 1617 and 1618, a record of the way one country squire spent his Sundays. From this we find that Assheton considered regular attendance at church a duty which he carefully performed, often twice on a Sunday and from the references made to the fact in the Diary it is clear that at his church at any rate the sermon was not a rare addition to the service. Yet Assheton was a man who certainly held no strict views about the Sunday in the puritanical sense, for not only did he frequently indulge rather freely in wine on the Sunday evening, but he sometimes devoted part of the day to business or sport. For example there is such an entry as the following for Sunday, July 27th, 1617: "Parson preached; after dinner, Mr. Leigh. To Worston. Spent xiid there merry".[1] The last somewhat cryptic phrase is a fairly common one in the journal to indicate what was probably a fairly mild state of intoxication. Deeper drinking led to the use of phrases like "very merry" and "more than merry" amongst others. On the afternoon of Sunday, September 7th, Assheton was busy with "copyhold business" although he had spent the morning at church.[2] Three weeks later on the Sunday there is the entry: "Word came to me that a stag was at the spring: Walbank took

---

[1] *Journal of Nicholas Assheton*, edit. F. R. Raines, p. 31.
[2] Ditto, p. 57.

his piece, and Miller his, but he was not to be found. Miller shot with Walbank at a mark and won."[1] On Sunday, July 19th, 1618, Assheton seems to have spent almost all the day in drinking and horseracing for money.[2] So we get a whimsical and contradictory picture of a man who was apparently devout enough at the appointed times of service—he records the text of the sermon in his journal more than once—but who evidently felt under no constraint with regard to his conduct on the rest of the Sunday. Such a man kept within the requirements of the letter if not the spirit of the regulations of the State and it was this fact which was causing an increasing number of the people to see that some stricter code of Sunday behaviour was necessary. The inconsistency of the conduct of a man like Assheton could only be regarded by the devoutly minded as a serious danger to the cause of true religion. No doubt some of the Puritans went to the opposite extreme but their narrowness and severity was calculated to do less harm than the example of a man like Assheton.

It will be well to contrast with Assheton a contemporary of his from the neighbouring county of Chester, John Bruen. He was in many ways typical of that class of Puritan who at this time were to be found *within* the ranks of the established Church. Bruen's biographer gives a picture of Bruen's conduct upon the Sunday which shows the example and influence men of his type were exerting at this time. The salient points in this account are as follows:—Mr. Bruen's house "was distant about a mile from the church, the way fair and large, so that he usually went afoot, calling all his family about him, leaving neither cook nor butler behind him, nor any of his servants, but two or three to make the doors, and tend the house, until their return. And then taking his tenants and neighbours, as they lay in the way, along with him, he marched on with a

[1] *Journal of Nicholas Assheton*, edit. F. R. Raines, p. 63.
[2] Ditto, p. 105.

joyful and cheerful heart, as a leader of the Lord's host, towards the house of God. . . . It was indeed his ordinary manner, to call his company near about him, and to join together with one heart and voice, to sing psalms as they went along. . . . His coming to the church with all his family, attendants and followers, was constantly before the beginning of prayers, or any part of divine service, that so he might more comfortably join with God's minister and people in confession of sins, in prayer and praise, reading and hearing of the word, singing of psalms, and partaking of the sacraments; all which he did perform with such a reverent attention and gracious affection, with so holy a carriage, and so good conscience, that as hereby he did much increase his own comfort, so was his godly example (no doubt) a great encouragement to many others, yea, a very spur and goad unto them, to be more religious and conscionable in God's worship and service. After prayers and sermon were ended, he seldom went home to dinner, but abode in the church to bestow himself and this interim in God's service, with such good people as were willing to stay with him. And this he did by repeating the sermon, which he had taken very exactly (as usually he did) with his own hand, and by singing of psalms, and by holy and wholesome conference in and about good things. And so waiting for the evening sacrifice, after he had with like care and conscience performed the public duties of the Sabbath in the same; he returned homeward with his company, with much comfort and joy in their hearts, endeavouring as they went along to increase their knowledge, faith and obedience, by repeating, and conferring of the evening sermon, and to enlarge their hearts in God's praises, by singing of psalms afresh, considering what great things had been done for them." [1]

Whatever may be said of the conduct of such a man at any rate he appears in the light of a *cheerful* Christian

[1] *Quoted in Journal of Assheton*, edit. F. R. Raines, pp. 3-4.

and usually the man of Puritan views is depicted as gloomy and cheerless. One imagines that Bruen enjoyed his Sundays more than Assheton, which is not to say that Assheton would have enjoyed being compelled to spend his Sunday as Bruen did.

Apart from the example of his own conduct a man like Bruen used his influence to persuade others to observe the Sunday more carefully. He persuaded a stranger who had been placed in his family to be trained in religious practices to adopt his mode of spending the Sunday.[1] On another occasion he speaks of "my cousin Dutton, being pressed and charged by some of great place to maintain his royalty of minstrelsy for piping and dancing on the Sabbath day, my minister, myself and my family were earnest against it and prevailed so far with my cousin Dutton, that he promised that all piping and dancing should cease on the Sabbath day, both forenoon and afternoon."[2]

It was the efficacy of the example and influence of men of the type of Bruen together with the diligence of certain of the magistrates such as we have noted in Lancashire that led those who desired to see the old holiday-holyday Sunday retained to make efforts to counteract the spreading of the stricter views with regard to Sunday conduct.

On Sunday, August 17th, 1617, James I was on his way from Scotland to England, travelling through Lancashire. Nicholas Assheton was one of those who were summoned to attend upon the King in Lancashire and his journal records the following for that date:—"August 17th. Houghton. We served the lords with biscuit, wine and jelly. The Bishop of Chester, Dr. Morton, preached before the King. To Dinner. About 4 o'clock there was a rushbearing and piping afore them, afore the King in the middle court; then to supper. Then, about ten or eleven o'clock, a masque

[1] *Journal of Assheton*, edit. F. R. Raines, p. 59.
[2] Ditto, p. 60.

of noblemen, knights, gentlemen and courtiers, afore the King, in the middle round, in the garden. Some speeches: of the rest, dancing." [1] Such a day was no doubt typical of many spent by James and his Court and accorded with his private and public attitude towards the spending of Sunday. The further conduct of the King is therefore quite logical and understandable. On the following Sunday James received a petition from certain of the inhabitants of the county desiring greater freedom to spend part of the Sunday in sport.

The reasons for this petition have, in part at any rate, already been dealt with. The magistrates had, as we have seen, sought to curtail the freedom of the people to amuse themselves as they liked on the Sunday. The fact that Lancashire was a county containing many Popish recusants and that it was believed that the leaders of these people tried to influence the general public to stay away from church and spend the time in dancing and sport had led the Bishop of the diocese to try to suppress this irreligous conduct. Consequently complaint against the bishop had been made already to the King. Now this complaint was renewed and a plea made for liberty to recreate themselves freely on the Sunday on the usual plausible lines that only so could servants and other hard working people obtain any exercise and amusement. James consulted the Bishop on the matter and the result was the issue of the King's declaration setting forth his commands in so far as he was concerned with the situation in Lancashire. [2] But the situation in Lancashire was, after all, not unique. In other parts of the country the magistrates and the more devoutly minded of the people had been trying to curb the more pronounced abuses of the Sunday and the people who, for any reason whatsoever, objected to this limitation of their old freedom were objecting to what was being done and so James was led in the

[1] *Journal of Assheton*, edit. F. R. Raines, p. 40.
[2] *Literature of the Sabbath Question* by R. Cox, Vol. I, p. 425: Barwick: *Life of Bishop Morton*, p. 80.

following May to re-issue his declaration in a somewhat fuller form and make it apply to the whole country.

This Declaration of Sports issued by James I from the royal manor of Greenwich on the twenty-fourth of May 1618 is a very important document and it will be well to reproduce it in detail here because not only does it set out the policy of James himself but it shows in what light the efforts of those who desired a stricter Sunday had been represented to the King. The declaration reads as follows:—[1]

"Whereas upon Our return the last year out of Scotland, we did publish our pleasure touching the recreations of our people in those parts under our hand, for some causes as thereunto moving, we have thought good to commend these our Directions then given in Lancashire with a few words thereunto added and most applicable to these parts of our realms, to be published to all our Subjects.

"Whereas we did justly in our progress through Lancashire rebuke some Puritans and precise people, and took order that the like unlawful carriage should not be used by any of them hereafter, in the prohibiting and unlawfully punishing of our Good people for using their lawful Recreations, and honest exercises upon Sundays and other Holy days, after the afternoon sermon or service: we now find that two sorts of people wherewith that country is much infested, (we mean Papists and Puritans) have maliciously traduced and calumniated those our just and honourable proceedings. And therefore lest our reputation might upon the one side (though innocently) have some aspersion laid upon it, and that upon the other part our good people in that country be misled by the mistaking and misinterpretation of our meaning: we have therefore thought good hereby to clear and make our pleasure to be manifested to all our good people in those parts.

[1] Reproduced in Cox *Literature of the Sabbath Question*, Vol. I, p. 444: Govett; *King's Book of Sports*, pp. 35-40.

"It is true that at our first entry to this crown and kingdom, we were informed, and that too truly, that our county of Lancashire abounded more in Popish Recusants than any County of England, and thus hath still continued since to our great regret, with little amendment, save that now of late, in our last riding through our said county, we find both by the report of the judges, and of the Bishop of that diocese, that there is some amendment now daily beginning, which is no small contentment to us.

"The report of this growing amendment among them, made us the more sorry, when with our own ears we heard the general complaint of our people, that they were barred from all lawful recreation, and exercise upon the Sunday's afternoon, after the ending of all divine service, which cannot but produce two evils: The one, the hindering of the conversion of many, whom their priest will take occasion hereby to vex, persuading them that no honest mirth or recreation is lawful or tolerable in our religion, which cannot but breed a great discontent in our people's hearts, especially of such as are peradventure upon the point of turning: the other inconvenience is, that this prohibition barreth the common and meaner sort of people from using such exercises as may make their bodies more able for war, when we or our successors shall have occasion to use them. And in place thereof sets up filthy tiplings and drunkenness and breeds a number of idle and discontented speeches in their alehouses. For when shall the common people have leave to exercise, if not upon the Sundays and holy days, seeing they must apply their labour and win their living in all working days?

"Our express pleasure therefore is, that the laws of our kingdom and canons of our church be as well observed in that county, as in all other places of this our kingdom. And on the other part, that no lawful recreation shall be barred to our good people, which shall not tend to the breach of our aforesaid laws, and canons of our church: which to express more particularly, Our pleasure is, That the Bishop, and all other inferior Churchmen, and Churchwardens, shall for their parts be careful and diligent, both to instruct the ignorant and convince and reform them that are misled in Religion, presenting them that will not conform themselves but obstinately stand out to Our judges and justices: whom we likewise command to put the Law in due execution against them.

"Our pleasure likewise is that the Bishop of that Diocese take the like straight order with all the Puritans and Precisians within the same, either constraining them to conform themselves, or to leave the county according to the laws of our kingdom and canons of our church, and so to strike equally on both hands, against the contemners of our Authority and adversaries of Our Church. And as for Our good people's lawful recreation, our pleasure likewise is, That after the end of Divine Service, Our good people be not disturbed, letted, or discouraged from any lawful recreation, such as dancing, either men or women, archery for men, leaping, vaulting, or any such harmless recreation, nor from having of May-games, Whitsun ales, and Morris dances, and the setting up of May-poles and other sports therewith used, so as the same be had in due and convenient time, without impediment or neglect of Divine Service: and that women shall have leave to carry rushes to the church for the decorating of it according to their old custom. But withall we do here account still as prohibited all unlawful games to be used upon Sundays only, as Bear and Bull-baitings, Interludes, and at all times in the meaner sort of people by law prohibited, bowling.

"And likewise we bar from this benefit and liberty, all such known recusants either men or women, as will abstain from coming to church or Divine Service, being therefore unworthy of any lawful recreation after the said service, that will not first come to the church, and serve God: prohibiting in like sort the said recreations to any that, though conform in Religion, are not present in the church at the service of God, before their going to the said Recreations. Our pleasure likewise is, That they to whom it belongeth in office, shall present and sharply punish all such as in abuse of this our liberty, will use these exercises before the ends of all Divine Services for that day. And we likewise straightly command, that every person shall resort to his own Parish Church to hear Divine Service, and each parish by itself to use the said recreations after Divine Service. Prohibiting likewise any offensive weapons to be carried or used in the said times of Recreations. And our pleasure is, that this our Declaration shall be published by order from the Bishop of the Diocese through all the Parish Churches, and that both our Judges of Our Circuit and our Justices of Our Peace be informed thereof."

This document of course did not indicate any fresh or startling development in the State policy for Sunday observance. It simply reiterated what had been the law of the State and of the Church since the early days of the Reformation. This indeed is its significance. It was a reactionary document in that it took no account, except in the way of prohibition, of the change in public opinion on the matter of Sunday observance which had been going on for at least forty years. By issuing it James made another mistake similar to that which he had made at the Hampton Court Conference. He stupidly blinded himself to the fact that in religious matters, as in political matters, the nation was unwilling to stand still. What had been good enough for their forefathers decidedly was not good enough for many of the subjects of James I.

After all it is difficult to see how James I could persuade himself that his declaration could do any good. The more irreligious of his subjects had been demonstrating for years, even before they became his subjects, that in spite of the law of the State and of the Church, they would not attend service regularly where they could avoid so doing and that to them the Sunday was a day to be spent in following their own devices. Many of the most deeply religious on the other hand, both within and without the State Church, together with many of those whose local responsibilities made them aware of the unsatisfactory conduct of so many on the Sunday, had been using their influence to bring about a stricter observance of the Sunday. All this we have seen illustrated from the history of Elizabeth's reign and the earlier years of James's reign. Neither class would be likely to change their attitude because James I chose to re-state the old position.

The attitude of James I, that is to say, savours of the attitude of a not-too-wise father in dealing with small children. If you are good children and go to church dutifully then, when you come out of church, you shall play certain games which are good for you before you go to bed. But unfortunately for James the children were growing up and they were not all inclined to agree that it was worth while being good children. At any rate, to change the figure, they were not all inclined to accept the pill in order to enjoy the jam. They were old enough to see through the device and, as older children will, they despised the one who tried to bluff them and were more inclined to respect, even if they resented, the authoritative command of the Puritan.

That is to say the Englishman of James I's reign had learnt in more directions than one to think for himself. No longer was he content to let all his affairs be ruled for him by a despotic government, however benevolent. He was intellectually keen enough and honest enough in many cases to see that mere attendance at church meant nothing. To the Government it meant much because above all it afforded an easy way of differentiating between the Papist and the Protestant. But unless the spiritual side of him bade him go to church because there he would find something that his nature would otherwise lack, the average citizen was likely to stay away if he could do so. If he could not manage to dodge attendance at church then his mind while there was no doubt much more occupied with his plans for amusing himself once the irksome attendance was over than in receiving any spiritual benefit.

Herein lies much of the justification as well as the explanation for the attitude taken up by those who advocated a stricter Sunday. Surrounded by so much likely to distract his attention from the sacredness of the day the average man was not likely to appreciate the real purpose or value of the Sunday they believed. But compel him to refrain both from work and from sport upon the Sunday and his mind would be at leisure to receive spiritual instruction and benefit. Future events were to justify, in a large measure at any rate, the theory.

The issue of the Declaration was unfortunate from another point of view. It tended to widen the breach between the Anglican and the dissenting Puritan. Quite wrongly, as this book has tried to show, James attempted to associate the idea of a strict observance of the Sunday solely with the teaching of the Puritans, meaning thereby the non-Anglican Puritans. In point of fact, as we have seen, many magistrates, certainly not all of whom were Puritan in any sense of the word, and many Puritans within the State Church were of the number of those who objected to that degree of freedom upon the Sunday which the Declaration permitted. But for the future it would be increasingly difficult for a person to advocate any stricter conduct upon the Sunday than that outlined in the Declaration without laying himself open to the charge of Puritanism implying thereby not merely a desire for a purer

7

moral standard but an attitude inimical to the State Church.

It seems strange that those who have seen fit to applaud the Declaration, because of the freedom it allowed the people to enjoy themselves, have ignored the reasons expressed in the document for granting this freedom. The "common and meaner sort of people"— for so James terms those of whom he is expressly thinking—are granted this liberty upon the Sunday because for six days of the week they must work hard every minute of the day. A six-days working week with compulsory church services on the Sunday and the opportunity after that to play, unless more work were required, as it might be. Not a particularly alluring prospect surely; hardly one that would be likely to appeal to the average citizen to-day. People conveniently ignore the definite stipulation of attendance at two church services before any recreation was allowed when they look back to what they are pleased to call the 'merry England' of pre-Puritan times.

Further, and this is also ignored by those who praise James's attitude, the freedom granted to the common people to indulge in sport was given from no altruistic motive, but in order that "such exercises may make their bodies more able for work". This, and a desire to present the Protestant religion in as favourable a light as possible and to make it seem no more irksome than the Roman form, together with a desire to content the ordinary people, motived James's declaration. Of any real desire to further the well-being of his subjects there is no evidence at all in the document.

One other point must be noticed and that is the way in which the Declaration deliberately libels the party who advocated a stricter Sunday by declaring that it was their policy which caused "filthy tiplings and drunkenness" and which produced "a number of idle and discontented speeches" in the alehouses. We have seen the magistrates having to deal with cases of riot and drunkenness in the reign of Elizabeth when the people were free enough to amuse themselves as they wished and when they certainly were not restrained by any Puritan influence from their sports. Then too James must have been strangely ignorant, if he were not purposely misrepresenting the Puritan influence, if he did not know that the last thing the advocates of the stricter Sunday would countenance would be drunkenness and idle gossip in alehouses.

While deploring the total misunderstanding of the situation which the issue of this Declaration demonstrated, the mistake must not be made, as it has sometimes been, of misreading the document itself. The Declaration is permissive, and not in any way a command that games shall be played on Sunday. James did not say that his people must dance and indulge in sport after the evening service; he only said that they must not be prevented from so doing if they desired to act in that way. Undoubtedly the tendency of the statement was to encourage the playing of games after the services for the day were over, but the individual was perfectly free to refrain from so doing if he wished.

The effect of the issue of this Declaration it is difficult if not impossible to estimate in detail. Certain broad conclusions however can be reached. Its chief result, undoubtedly, as has already been suggested, was to deepen and widen the cleavage between the State Church and the Dissenting Puritans. It made the question of Sunday observance a more prominent issue in the eyes of the people of the country and thereby possibly did harm rather than good. Some have thought that if James had not brought the issue into the open in this way the influence of those who desired a stricter observance of the Sunday would gradually have won people over to their view.[1] The fact that this was considered to be a decided possibility is seen by the approval which an advocate of the less-strict

[1] See for example S. R. Gardener *History of England*, Vol. III, p. 248.

Sunday like Peter Heylyn gave to the Declaration
when he called it "the first blow, in effect, which had
been given, in all his (i.e. James's) time, to the new
Lord's-day Sabbath, then so much applauded."[1] Now
that the blow had been struck the advocates of the
stricter Sunday would be only the more determined to
press their theories and would almost of necessity be
inclined, if not bound, to make their demands more
strict. This point needs to be kept in mind when any
idea of censuring the ultra-severe Sunday which some
of the Puritans advocated is entertained. By refusing
to make any allowance for the wishes and claims of
those who desired a more reverent Sunday, James
deliberately drove such people to adopt in their turn a
theory about the Sunday which had no place in it for
the ideas which James advocated.

In actual practice the result of the issue of the
Declaration made but little difference in all proba-
bility. Some of the magistrates were not now so strict
as they had been to enforce a more reverent Sunday.
We have seen for example how in Lancashire they had
to modify their regulations in order to bring them into
line with the King's Declaration and there are very
few cases recorded of prosecutions under those regulations which, as the editor of the records states, may be
due to the issue of the Declaration.[2] But on the other
hand it is not likely that many, if any, of those who had
been influenced by the example of those who advocated
and practised a more reverent Sunday would be led
to change their views because of what the Declaration
said. Rather, in some cases at any rate, people who had
not thought much of the matter before but whose attention had now been forcibly drawn to it would tend to
study the issue for themselves and would decide that
there was more that appealed to them in the newer
view of the way in which Sunday should be spent than

---

[1] *History of the Sabbath* by P. Heylyn, Bk. II, p. 261.
[2] *Manchester Sessions*, edit. E. Axon, Vol. I, p. xxiii.

in the old reactionary view of James. Certainly, as later events show, the Declaration did not achieve the purpose which its author had in mind and it stands as an example of an unwise attempt to ignore the advance of public opinion upon a vital question and impose upon the people an outworn conception which progressive minds could not accept.

If James had imagined that his Declaration would put an end to non-attendance at church or to the profanation of the hours of Divine Service he must have been disappointed. The local records still testify to breaches of the law in these particulars. For example even in Lancashire itself at the Manchester Sessions, held on May 4th, 1620, the court had to deal with five alehouse-keepers of Newton, Bury and Manchester who "suffered divers persons to drink and be disordered in their houses in time of divine service upon the Sabbath day." They were sentenced to three days imprisonment and disqualified from holding a license to sell ale and beer.[1] The Worcester County Quarter Sessions, in April, 1620, had to deal with a charge of "extraordinary drinking and quarrelling on the Sabbath day, that is on Sunday the 7th of the month of April."[2] In Yorkshire at Thirske in October, 1621 a man and his wife were charged with "making a drinking" on Sunday during service time when "there was one so drunk that he drew forth a knife and would have killed divers but that good help was made, it being very ordinary with them to make drinkings on the Sabbath day."[3] A more serious state of affairs still is indicated a few years later in the record for the Yorkshire Quarter Sessions held at Richmond in 1625 which reads: "The Jury further present Jas. Cotes of Arde-town in Arkengarth-dale, one of the Churchwardens there, and an alehouse-keeper, for keeping disorder in his house and playing at cards with the Parish Clerk, and other disordered

[1] *Manchester Sessions*, edit. Axon, Vol. I, p. 114.
[2] *Worcester County Records*, edit. Bund, p. 324.
[3] *Quarter Sessions Records*, edit. Atkinson, Vol. III, p. 125.

company, on the Sabbath day during Divine Service and Evening prayer."[1] Not only those whose duty it was to enforce the law but the ordinary people themselves frowned upon such desecration of a day which more and more people were considering to have a peculiar religious significance. Thus we find that the Worcestershire justices in 1621 received a "Petition of the inhabitants of Bayton . . . shewing that Wm. Bryan and Thomas Morley of Bayton, alesellers, continually harbour vagrant and lewd persons in their houses during divine service."[2]

James I indeed cannot be said to have set his subjects a very good example in this respect for it is recorded that just about the time of the issue of the Declaration of Sports the royal carriages made such a disturbance and noise in passing through the City of London during the time of Divine Service that the Lord Mayor had them stopped. The officers in charge of the carriages complained to the King who is reported to have been very enraged and to have sent a warrant to the Lord Mayor to let the carriages proceed. The Lord Mayor did so, remarking: "While it was in my power, I did my duty; but that being taken away by a higher power, it is my duty to obey."[3] Undoubtedly the Lord Mayor was more in touch with, and better able to interpret, the opinion of the people with regard to Sunday observance than was his King.

---

[1] *Quarter Sessions Records*, edit. Atkinson, Vol. III, p. 250.
[2] *Report of the Historical Manuscripts Commission for* 1901, Vol. I, p. 303.
[3] Reported in *Works of Disraeli*, Vol. VI, p. 426.

CHAPTER VIII

THE ATTITUDE OF PARLIAMENT TO SUNDAY OBSERVANCE
DURING THE FIRST THIRTY YEARS OF THE SEVENTEENTH
CENTURY

REFERENCE was made at the end of Chapter III to the
fact that Parliament, during the latter part of the reign
of Elizabeth, gave indications that its wishes were in
the direction of a stricter observance of the Sunday
than that indicated by the attitude of the Queen.
Parliament, however, in the reign of Elizabeth was,
particularly in religious matters, usually very deferen-
tial to the Queen, but with the coming of James to the
English throne the English Parliament became much
more assertive and very much more the mouthpiece of
the people's wishes. We should expect, therefore, that
Parliament would have much more to say about this
question of Sunday observance in the reigns of James I
and Charles I than it had had previously, and the facts
support the supposition. This again is an aspect of
the subject which has received very scanty treatment
in the past and, consequently, very few probably have
realized that whatever might be the attitude of the
monarch and the State Church to the existing method of
keeping the Sunday, Parliament was not by any means
satisfied. The House of Commons was in a far better
position to sense and interpret the wishes of the people
than the monarch or the bishops, and therefore its
attitude is very significant. Unfortunately the details
of the various Bills which were introduced on the subject
have not been preserved for us, nor, in most cases, have
we the details of the debates upon such Bills. But such

particulars as we have preserved for us, together with the deductions which seem warrantable from these facts, will now be set down.

In January 1606 a Bill "for the better observing and keeping holy the Sabbath days or Sundays" was introduced into the House of Commons[1] and before the end of February it had passed through all its stages in the Lower House and had been sent on to the House of Lords. Very little of any debate on the Bill in the House of Commons has survived, but one member referred to the bad example set in the matter of Sunday observance by the Justices of the Peace, and other members stated that, in their opinion, cessation from work upon the Sunday was sufficient recreation for people.[2] This Bill reached the Committee stage in the House of Lords, but on the day Parliament was prorogued, in May, the Archbishop of Canterbury reported the Bill amongst others which had not been proceeded with.[3] The House of Lords had not had a very long time—some three months—in which to consider the Bill, and it may have been lack of time which prevented their agreeing to it. But more probably they were not as yet convinced of the necessity of strengthening the law on the matter. On the other hand, although we have not got the details of the Bill, from the title of the measure it is clear that the House of Commons—which, need it be said, would hardly be a predominantly Puritan House in any sense of that word—was convinced that the proclamation of James and the Canon of the State Church on the matter had not done by any means all that needed to be done to reform the existing abuses connected with the Sunday. That is to say, if the House of Commons had been able to have its way in 1606 the Sunday would have been more strictly observed from that time onwards than either the King

---

[1] *Journals of the House of Commons*, Vol. I, p. 260.
[2] *Common's Journals I.* 269.
[3] *Journals of the House of Lords*, Vol. II, p. 444.

or the authorities of the Anglican Church thought necessary.

In April 1614 another Bill "for the better observing and keeping holy the Sabbath-day or Sunday" was introduced in the House of Commons.[1] A few details are given of one of the debates upon this bill from which it appears that one member moved to have football included amongst the things not permitted upon the Sunday, while several members wanted a clause putting in to prevent carriers travelling on the Sunday—an old Elizabethan source of complaint. Two members pleaded that the Bill should forbid resort being made to alehouses on the Sunday, their purpose apparently being to keep such places closed for the whole of the day and not merely during the times of Divine Worship. One member wanted a clause "against writing in offices and hearing of causes" and he was supported by another who moved "against working on the Sabbath, wherein the lawyers most faulty".[2] All this is most interesting as showing the lines upon which the members' thoughts were working. Clearly the Bill aimed at limiting, at any rate, the number of games which were permissible on the Sunday, and equally clearly there were at least some members of the House who were in accord with those Justices of the Peace and devoutly minded people who, on the grounds of morality, if not on spiritual grounds, desired to see an end put to the drunkenness of many people upon the Sunday and to the way the day was used by many people for transacting their ordinary business. By the 21st of May the Bill had completed all its stages in the House of Commons, and before the end of the month the Archbishop of York was reporting to the House of Lords the view of the committee of the Lords which had considered the Bill. Evidently the committee was sympathetic to the Bill, for the Archbishop said that:

[1] *Commons' Journals I*, p. 467.
[2] Ditto, p. 476.

"The Lords' Committee did hold the drift and purpose thereof to be good, and to tend to the Glory of God; howbeit, for that they conceived the same fit in some points to be reformed" they desired a conference on the Bill, with a committee of the House of Commons. This was agreed upon but either the terms of the conference were misunderstood by the Lower House or they were unwilling to alter the Bill because the Archbishop of York had later to report to the House of Lords that the conference had broken down, because the representatives of the House of Commons upon it said that they had no authority to discuss changes, but only to report what was said to their own House.[1] This seems to have been the end of the matter, and Parliament was dissolved three days later.

This much, however, marks an advance. The House of Lords was now disposed to think that something ought to be done to ensure the better observance of the Sunday—a significant fact in itself. It was not prepared to go as far as the House of Commons in the matter, but again that is only what we should expect. Anything that savoured of Puritanism in any way was not likely to receive the approval of the bishops and the majority of the peers. That they went as far as they did in commending the Bill shows that they cannot have considered it to be prompted by any Puritan motives, but that they, like the Commons, were aware that all was not well with the way in which many of the people kept the Sunday.

In February 1621 the House of Commons tried once more and a Bill was introduced "for punishment of divers abuses on the Sabbath day, called Sunday".[2] One of the debates on this Bill caused an angry scene which led to one of the members, named Shepherd, having to withdraw from the House, and later he was declared to have forfeited his seat. Shepherd roused the temper of the House because he opposed the Bill on

[1] *Lords' Journals II*, p. 714.
[2] *Commons' Journals I*, p. 514.

the grounds that in the title the word "Sabbath" ought not to be used because it stood for Saturday; that the Bill prohibited dancing which ought first to be condemned as unlawful by the Divines; that the Bill was contrary to the royal Declaration of Sports; and finally that the Bill was the work of a Puritan and, indeed, of "a Sectary and Disturber of the Peace".[1] Sir George Moore seems to have voiced fairly accurately the feeling of the House when he protested that "to inveigh, in such a bitter manner, against this bill (where, in 27. Elizabeth a more strict passed) (was) not sufferable".

Several points of interest arise from this incident. First of all the reference to the use of the term "Sabbath" reminds us that by that time that word was becoming associated in the minds of many people with the Puritans, meaning thereby in this connection all those who desired to enforce a more strictly-kept Sunday. This was the outcome of the fact that those who wrote in favour of a stricter view of the Sunday, basing their arguments upon the fourth Commandment, almost invariably used the word "Sabbath" for the Sunday. It had not always been so. The early Protestants used the word "Sabbath" without in any way indicating their desire to enforce the rules of the Jewish Sabbath. For example, as has been shown in this book, the word "Sabbath" appeared in the King's Book of 1543 and was used by Archbishops Cranmer and Parker. But since any marked difference of opinion had appeared over the way in which Sunday should be kept, the term "Sabbath" had been avoided by that party which was in favour of allowing as much latitude as possible to the people with regard to their conduct on Sunday, provided always that they attended church. The fact, therefore, that the House of Commons put the word "Sabbath" into their Bill is suggestive of the fact that they were anxious to place some restrictions upon the license of the day and that in some sense, at any rate,

[1] *Commons' Journals I*, p. 521.

they were looking to the Fourth Commandment for guidance in their plan.

Another point to notice is that the Bill clearly shows that the House of Commons did not agree with the royal Declaration of Sports, another proof that James I had failed to interpret the change that was going on in the country in people's views on this subject, as on so many subjects, and that the House of Commons was more closely in touch with the public temper than the King. Also the reference made to the Bill passed in Elizabeth's reign is interesting because, provided of course that we can accept Sir George Moore's comparison as an accurate one, it shows that that Bill would have gone much further than Elizabeth desired. Indeed, that was why it did not become law. That such was the case and that again the House of Commons knew better than the Queen what the country required, the available evidence for that period seems to show as has been explained in an earlier chapter.

To return now to the Bill of 1621 we find that it eventually passed the House of Commons without a dissentient vote. The House of Lords apparently could find nothing to object to in the Bill this time except the use of the word "Sabbath" which they disliked "because divers incline now to Judaism"[1] and the Lower House met them on this point by agreeing to substitute the term "Lord's Day" for "Sabbath". This Bill, therefore, received the approval of both Houses of Parliament but, as might be expected, James I refused to accept it and so it never became law. But nothing could show more clearly that it was only James himself who prevented the policy of the State on the matter of Sunday observance coming more into line with the wishes of so many of his subjects, many of whom would have scorned and repudiated the term Puritan in whatever sense of the word it had been applied to them.

[1] *Commons' Journal I*, p. 628.

Undaunted by their failures to get their wishes made law, the House of Commons, four days after the beginning of a new Parliament, in 1624, brought in "the Bill of the Sabbath; which passed both Houses last Convention in Parliament, and hath ever, since 27 Elizabeth passed this House".[1] Within a fortnight it had successfully completed all its stages in both Houses and only required the King's approval to become law. The only point upon which any discussion is reported is one about the exercise of arms after the evening service. It was, of course, an old custom and, indeed, an old law that people should practice archery after the evening service on Sunday, and in the House of Lords the question was raised as to whether this Act would forbid military exercise on Sunday. The matter was referred to the Judges for a ruling and their decision was: "That the exercise of Arms is not a sport forbidden by the Law, and so not within the Act".[2]

James I as before refused to give his assent to this measure on the grounds that "it contradicted his own allowance of lawful recreations, and that this act would give the Puritans their way, who think religion consists in two sermons a day".[3] In referring to this Bill in his private diary Walter Yonge, who was a member of Parliament for Honiton, a Justice of the Peace, and one who could be counted as a moderate Puritan, who was loyal to the State Church, calls it "a good Bill . . . against revels and for the sanctifying of the Sabbath".[4] Evidently, therefore, the Bill was one which satisfied those who, either as magistrates or from religious conviction, regarded the freedom granted by the King's Book of Sports as unsatisfactory. On the other hand, the Bill cannot in any sense of the word have been a fanatical measure or it would not so easily and quickly have passed through the two Houses, par-

[1] *Commons' Journals I*, p. 671.
[2] *Lords' Journals*, Vol. III, p. 252.
[3] Letter of Edw. Nicholas to John Nicholas—*Cal. State Papers*, Dom 1624, Vol. CLXV No. 61.
[4] *Diary of Walter Yonge*, edit. G. Roberts, p. 75.

ticularly through the House of Lords. We may assume that it received there the assent of the bishops or the majority of them, or surely some record of their disagreement would have been preserved. The history of this Bill seems to be but another example of the way in which James I persistently flouted the wishes of his people as expressed through Parliament.

The determination of the House of Commons to get some measure to increase the sanctity of the Sunday upon the Statute Book is shown by the fact that the first item in the Journal of that House for the first Parliament of Charles I in 1625 is the introduction of "An Act for punishing of divers abuses committed on (the) Lord's day, called Sunday". It will be noted that the term "Sabbath" has been dropped from the title as it had been in 1621, although it had re-appeared in 1624. This Bill again passed both Houses with apparently little or no trouble, and it received the royal assent and so became law. Probably, judging by his conduct and views at a later date, Charles I was no more in agreement with the measure than his father had been, but so early in his reign Charles was not in a position to quarrel with the wishes of Parliament particularly when, as he must have well known, they were wishes which for a quarter of a century Parliament had tried to make law. Sir John Bramston says that by agreeing to this measure Charles "testified his zeal for religion".[1] If others like Sir John took that view then, and Sir John apparently still held that view when he wrote the statement in 1683, many were destined to change it or to conclude that Charles had lost his zeal before very many years had passed.

The details of this Act, which presumably embodies some, but probably not all, of the things which Parliament had been seeking to make law for so long must now be considered. The Act was not a long one and the essential points in it are these:[2]

[1] *Autobiography of Sir John Bramston*, p. 41.
[2] I Charles I, Cap I.

"Forasmuch as there is nothing more acceptable to God than the true and sincere service and worship of him according to His Holy Will, and that the holy keeping of the Lord's Day is a principal part of the true service of God, which in very many places of this Realm hath been and now is profaned and neglected by a disorderly sort of people in exercising and frequenting bear-baiting, bull-baiting, interludes, common plays, and other unlawful exercises and pastimes upon the Lord's Day; and for that many quarrels, bloodsheds, and other great inconveniences have grown by the resort and concourse of people going out of their own parishes to such disordered and unlawful exercises and pastimes, neglecting Divine Service both in their own parishes and elsewhere; Be it enacted . . . that . . . there shall be no meetings, assemblies or concourse of people out of their own parishes on the Lord's Day, within this Realm of England or any the Dominions thereof, for any Sports and Pastimes whatsoever; nor any bear-baiting, bull-baiting, interludes, common plays or other unlawful exercises and pastimes, used by any person or persons within their own parishes; and that every person or persons offending in any the premises shall forfeit for every offence three shillings four pence, the same to be employed and converted to the use of the poor of the parish where such offence shall be committed". This act was at first to be in force only to the end of the first session of the next Parliament, but it was then continued, as it was again in 1640.

If this act embodies all that the previous Bills upon the matter had contained, one wonders why James I refused to agree to them, except in so far that he probably considered that the mere fact of passing any law on the matter of Sunday observance was an indication that his own Declaration had failed in its express purpose. For this Act really conflicts but little with the Declaration. The things which it prohibits James had prohibited. There is really no new regulation in this Act. Yet the spirit of the Act is undoubtedly stricter, and its chief value for us in estimating the conditions prevailing at the time lies in the preamble, as is so often the case with an old statute. That makes it quite clear that the Declaration of 1618 had done no good in the matter of improving the sanctity of the Sunday, and nobody, surely, could really have expected it would. The preamble simply illustrates, but illustrates very forcibly, what we have already seen illustrated in other directions, namely, the fact that those who had little or no regard for the holiness of the day would not be content with the limits either of time or of scope for their amusements which the Declaration imposed upon them but would be satisfied with nothing less than the whole day in which to do just whatever they liked.

This Act does not prohibit all games upon the Sunday, and therefore would not do all that those who based their demands upon a strict interpretation of the fourth commandment would wish. But on the other hand, if only this Act could be enforced it would do a great deal to remedy the most glaring cases of abuse. Particularly by preventing the people from roaming about from one parish to another on the Sunday, many of the disgraceful scenes, such as we have seen the people of Worcestershire complaining of some eight years previously, would be ended. Nothing fresh is done to deal with the question of excessive drinking on the Sunday, so that the member who desired the total closing of the alehouses on Sunday in 1614 would not think the Bill went far enough. Yet the Act would demonstrate to the country the fact that Parliament was determined not to allow a state of license upon the Sunday, a state which many had no doubt been encouraged to expect by the terms of the Declaration of 1618 and the evident failure to enforce the existing regulations, at any rate in some parts of the country.

But it seems certain that this Act did not contain all

that had been in the minds of previous parliaments. We saw, for example, that in the debates of 1614 the matter of Sunday labour was raised, and this finds no place in the Act of 1625. Possibly the members of Parliament who were most keen on reform had learned wisdom by their many attempts to get a measure on the Statute Book and had realized, as most reformers have to do, that an imperfect act was better than none at all and had concentrated first upon a measure which, as we have seen, did little but reinforce the existing lawful position, knowing that to put the seal of Parliament to that much measure of restriction would be a step in the direction in which they desired to travel. Then, emboldened by the fact that at last some of their work had been accomplished, they tried again two years later.

The "Act for the further reformation of sundry abuses committed on the Lord's Day, commonly called Sunday" which was obtained in 1627 seems to have caused very little controversy. Yet, from the social standpoint at any rate, this Act was a very important one, because for the first time the Legislature adopted the principle that Sunday labour, in some of its branches at any rate, was a thing to be forbidden. Here again Parliament was only following out what had been the desire of many people for a long time. The chief points to notice in this Act are the following. It said:[1]

"Forasmuch as the Lord's Day, commonly called Sunday, is much broken and profaned by Carriers, Waggoners, Carters, Wain-men, Butchers and Drovers of Cattle to the great dishonour of God, and reproach of religion: Be it enacted . . . That no Carrier with any horse or horses, nor Waggon-men with any waggon or waggons, nor Carmen with any cart or carts, nor Wain-men with any wain or wains, nor Drovers with any cattle shall . . . by themselves, or any other, travel upon the said day, upon pain that every person

[1] 3 Charles I, C.I.

or persons so offending shall lose and forfeit twenty shillings for every such offence: or: if any Butcher, by himself or any other for him by his privity or consent, shall . . . kill or sell any victual upon the said day, that then every such Butcher shall forfeit and lose for every such offence the sum of six shillings and eight pence ".

Thus two long-standing complaints were dealt with. We have noticed before that the waggoners and the butchers were the source of complaint in various places because they disturbed the peace of the Sunday. The clatter of the carts over the cobble-stones of the towns, together with the noisy shouts of the drivers would, in those days, no doubt be as great a distraction to a worshipping congregation as the rumble and rasp of ancient tram-cars over obsolete tram-lines can be to-day —indeed it would be much worse, because to-day the one sound is usually intermingled with others only a degree less strident, and we are a generation inured to noise, whereas in the former case there would be little else to break the peace of the Sunday quietude. There is to-day still a class of butcher who seems to think it necessary to attract attention to his beef by his brawl. One would imagine he must be a survival of the Elizabethan and Jacobean race of butchers, judging by the fact that they seem so often to be referred to as disturbers of the peace of their fellow citizens. The narrowness of the Shambles, as can still be seen in ancient towns where the name has persisted, where the butcher did his work and sold his meat and which was also a public thoroughfare, would also increase the offensiveness of any pursuit of a trade of that nature on the Sunday.

Thus cautiously, as befitted a body that was gradually feeling its power and learning by bitter experience how to gain more, and logically Parliament was supporting the doctrine that Sunday should at any rate be a day of rest and peace undisturbed by the thoughtless revelry or the noisy labour of those who had no regard either for the sanctity of the day or for the quietude of their fellows. Parliament, that is to say, was seeking to establish the Sunday as a day of Rest, and in so doing they were conferring an immeasurably great boon upon the people. But such a position was not as yet firmly established. Had Parliament been able to continue its work, either by further legislation where it thought necessary, or by measures to see that the existing legislation was obeyed, perhaps all that was still necessary to achieve such an end might have been secured with little or no fuss or opposition. One cannot say. What actually happened was that Parliament soon ceased, for that period which historians have labelled "The Eleven Years' Tyranny", to control the affairs of the land. When Parliament met again after that period of misrule, it had to face the question of Sunday observance afresh in the light of the events of the preceding decade.

CHAPTER IX

THE years between the legislation dealing with the observance of Sunday which was enacted in 1625 and 1627, and the calling of the Long Parliament in 1640, were years in which the gulf between those who advocated a Sunday devoted entirely to spiritual things, and those who were satisfied with a mere perfunctory attendance at church, was widened and deepened. That this should be so is quite understandable. They were the years in which more and more people were ranging themselves either upon the side of the King or upon the side which would exalt the power of Parliament and through Parliament of the people. For well-known reasons, which need not therefore be detailed here, the tendency was for the King to receive the support of and in return to uphold those in the State Church who were most disposed to what, for want of a better term, is generally called the High Church view of religion. Similarly, the Puritans, both within and without the State Church, were generally ranked upon the side of Parliament. The doctrine of the strict observance of the Sunday was being regarded more and more as a distinctive Puritan doctrine even though many who held it, in part at any rate if not completely, would not come within any definition of that term. On the other hand James I had clearly shown that his view of the Sunday was that people should be free to enjoy themselves much as they wished provided only that they attended Church and Charles I was soon to make it clear that he held the same view. Supporters of the almost unlimited power of the King as they were, and suspicious of and hostile to the increasing influence of the Puritans, the High Church Party in the Anglican Church would have been almost bound to support the attitude of the King on the Sunday question even if its sympathies and beliefs had not tended to a great extent in that direction. So the matter of Sunday observance became one of many points at issue between the rival camps in the years preceding the Civil War.

Those who wished to make Sunday a day of rest from all labour believed that such was the intent behind the Act of 1627 and they read more into that Act than others were inclined to allow. The strict Puritan of course needed no Act of Parliament to demonstrate to him that Sunday labour was wrong even though the worker was neither carrier nor butcher. But others, particularly all good citizens who had the amenities of their town at heart, not unnaturally interpreted the spirit of that Act as being opposed to any and every form of unnecessary work. That very much of such work was still done, and that some at any rate in positions of authority did not agree with it, is very well illustrated by an order issued by the Lord Mayor of London in April, 1629. It is worth while reproducing this order in full because of the picture that it gives of conditions in London on the Sunday at that time. The order reads thus:[1]

"Whereas I am credibly informed that notwithstanding divers good laws provided for the keeping of the Sabbath-day holy, according to the express command of Almighty God, divers inhabitants and other persons of the City, and other places, having no respect of duty towards God, and his Majesty, or his laws, but in contempt of them, do commonly and of custom greatly profane the Sabbath day, in buying, selling, uttering, and venting their wares and commodities upon

[1] Rushworth's *Historical Collections*, Part 2, Vol. I, p. 22.

that day for their private gain. Also innholders suffering markets to be kept by carriers, in most rude and
profane manner, in selling victuals to hucksters,
chandlers, and all other comers. Also carriers, carmen,
cloth-workers, water-bearers, and porters carrying of
burdens, and watermen plying their wares, and divers
other working in their ordinary callings. And likewise
that I am further informed, that vintners, alehouse-
keepers, tobacco and strong-water-sellers, greatly profane the Sabbath-Day, by suffering company to sit
drinking and bibbing in their houses on that day; and
likewise divers by cursing and swearing, and suchlike
behaviour, contrary to the express commandment of
Almighty God, his Majesty's laws in that behalf, and all
good government. For the reformation whereof, I do
hereby require, and in his Majesty's name straightly
command all his Majesty's loving subjects whatsoever:
and also all constables . . ." to find and apprehend and
bring before the Lord Mayor or some justice of the
peace "all and every such person or persons as shall be
found to offend in any of these kinds."

Such a condition of affairs as was outlined there was
surely justification enough for those who demanded
that further action ought to be taken to remedy the
abuses of the Sunday. Socially, quite apart from any
religious tenet, it was a wrong state of affairs that so
many people should be trading and working exactly as
they did upon the other six days of the week. It was a
far worse state of affairs than any aspect of Sunday
trading to-day because to-day the law does ensure that
the shop-keeper gives his assistants at least one half-
holiday in the week. There was no such protection for
them in Stuart times. It will be seen too that not only
must apprentices and journey-men have been at work
along with their masters in the shops but servants in the
inns and alehouses and labourers in many other trades
were kept employed. Ironical as it seems the freedom

to recreate oneself as one wished, within certain limits, upon the Sunday, which the King and the High Church party advocated, was deliberately mis-interpreted by many as a freedom to force one's employees to work. Attention has been drawn to this before but even at the risk of labouring the point it must be emphasized again because it is usually ignored in any reference to the way in which Sunday was spent at this time. Everyone was not able, even though the King and the State Church said he might, to spend his time after Divine Service in healthy sport or recreation—in many cases he had to spend even the time when he should have been at Divine Service in driving his master's waggon, or tending his master's stall in the market, or serving in his master's shop or in doing a hundred and one menial tasks. Those who would put an end to the right of those who wished to play upon part of the Sunday would also put an end to the misery of those who, against their wishes no doubt in many cases, were compelled to work through a part or the whole of Sunday.

That Sunday trading in totally unnecessary directions was not confined to London the records of other places would show. For example in 1631 the Worcestershire Quarter Sessions had to deal with a shoemaker because "being a Sunday he sold to one Henry Barnes a pair of shoes and other goods to divers persons unknown thereby on the said day carrying on his craft and occupation contrary to the form of the Statute."[1] One of the dangers that has always resulted when one individual trader breaks the law with regard to the conditions under which he is allowed to trade is illustrated by the fact that three other shoemakers of the same place are charged at the same time with similar offences. If one shoemaker traded all must or lose some custom.

The attention of the country generally was, however,

[1] *Worcester County Records*, edit. Bund, p. 481.

much more fixed upon the matter of Sunday amusements than upon the question of Sunday work. This was particularly so round about 1633 and 1634, due to certain events which occurred in the West of England. The events must therefore next be reviewed in some detail. It seems that complaints had been made about the disorder which occurred at Wakes and Revels and Church Ales and other Church feasts, which were usually held on the Sunday. Before discussing the points at issue it may be well to explain just what these various festival occasions were.

The day upon which the Saint, in whose name the church had been dedicated, was remembered, was marked by special celebrations, known as Feasts, or Wakes, or Revels. It had become customary, even when the day did not fall upon a Sunday, to hold such Feasts upon the Sunday nearest to the actual day of the Saint in question. Church Ales were special Sunday festivals organized to bring in money for some Parish object, such as the renovation or decoration of the church, and not only did the people amuse themselves upon the village green or within the churchyard after the services were over, but they consumed very often large quantities of ale. Similarly Clerk-Ales were organized to supplement the payments made to the Parish Clerk, and Bid-Ales were used to provide money for some poor inhabitant of the village or town. All these days were welcomed by many people as affording an exceptional opportunity for sport and recreation and also for heavy drinking. Consequently, as has been noted earlier, these occasions were often the scenes of disturbances and many magistrates and law-abiding citizens were therefore anxious to restrict and abolish such festivals.

In 1632 Sir Thomas Richardson the Lord Chief Justice, and Baron Denham at the Somerset Assizes issued an order declaring that: "Revels, Church-Ales, Clerks-Ales and all other public Ales be henceforth utterly suppressed."[1] They also directed that this order should be read in every Parish Church on certain Sundays. Their action, although it seems to have been done at the request of a number of the people of the district, apparently greatly incensed Archbishop Laud, particularly because of the instructions that the order should be read in the churches, although such was in those days the usual method of making public any authoritative pronouncement. Richardson defended his action on the grounds not only that it was done at the request of a number of magistrates but also that there were strong precedents for it. He cited a similar order made at Bridgwater by the Lord Chief Justice of the time in 1594 and 1596 and of the magistrates in Devon in 1599. Also he quoted an Order made in 1615 at Exeter which referred to several manslaughters having been committed at certain Church Ales and to the evidence which there was "of the continual profanation of God's Sabbath at these and such like unlawful meetings," an order made by two of the Judges at Exeter in 1627 prohibiting all Ales and revels: and an order made in Somerset in the same year in the same tenure.[2]

Laud wrote to the Bishop of Bath and Wells to inquire whether any disorder did accompany the celebration of these feasts which would justify Richardson's action. In his reply the Bishop says that he has consulted some seventy-two of his clergy on the matter and that he summarizes their conclusions on the matter of Feasts as follows:[3]

"First, that they have been kept not only this last year, but also for many years before, as long as they have lived in their several parishes without any disorders. Secondly that upon the Feast days (which are for the most part everywhere upon Sundays) the service of the Church hath been more solemnly performed, and

[1] Prynne: *Canterburies Doome*, pp. 131-2.
[2] Ditto, pp. 144-146.
[3] Ditto, pp. 141-142.

the Church hath been better frequented both in the Forenoon and in the afternoon, than upon any Sunday in the year. Thirdly that they have not known or heard of any disorders in the neighbouring towns where the like feasts are kept. Fourthly, that the people do very much desire the continuance of the feasts. Lastly, that all these ministers are of opinion, that it is fit and convenient these feast days should be continued, for a memorial of the dedications of their several Churches, for the civilizing of the people, for their lawful recreations, for the composing of differences by occasion of the meeting of friends, for the increase of love and unity, as being feasts of charity, for the relief of the poor, the richer for keeping them in a manner open house, and for many other reasons."

The Bishop himself quite evidently concurs in the opinions of these clergymen of his diocese. He states that the Feasts are almost always held on the Sunday because "on the week days the people have not had leisure to celebrate these Feasts." There is a striking contradiction between the view of the magistrates who petitioned Richardson in the first place to prohibit such Feasts and the declaration in the letter that no disorders ever accompany such Feasts. It is too glaring a contradiction to permit of any explanation other than that one or the other party was deliberately misrepresenting the facts and all the evidence points to the clergy as the guilty group. One cannot imagine the whole bench of magistrates, and the request to Richardson is spoken of as being unanimous, to have been Puritan or that being so they would be able to delude two of the King's Judges. On the other hand the letter itself furnishes sufficient evidence to show that the clergy had every inducement to ignore any signs of disorder. Too often to-day clergymen are inclined to overlook methods at Church Bazaars which savour very much of breaking the law with regard to

gambling and it is understandable, although not
necessarily excusable, that the Stuart clergy were not
anxious to tamper with very lucrative methods of
raising necessary church funds. The reasons advanced
by the clergy in favour of the Feasts are so delightfully
altruistic that they savour strongly of what the Psy-
chologists have taught us to call rationalization. Then,
too, many of the clergy were anxious to support anything that would further alienate the Puritans and, to
continue quoting from the Bishop's letter, "some of the
ministers who were with me have ingenuously confessed that if the people should not have their honest
and lawful recreations upon Sundays after evening
Prayer, they would go either into tipling houses, and
there upon their ale-benches talk of matters of the
Church or State or else into Conventicles." One cannot either admire, or place much reliance on the value
of the judgment of, men who upheld these Feasts
because thereby they obtained good congregations on
at least one day of the year and who felt that their own
influence and teaching would avail nothing to keep
people either from the alehouse or the Conventicle.

The upshot of this letter and the interference of Laud
was that Richardson in the following year had to
revoke his order very much against his will. The manner in which he did so showed his own convictions on
the matter to be unchanged and was such as to bring
him into increased disgrace at the Court. He declared
to the magistrates: "that he thought he had done God,
the King and his country, good service by that order
that he and his brother Denham had made . . . but
that it had been misreported to his majesty . . .
accordingly (says he) 'I do, as much as in me lies,
reverse it, declaring the same to be null and void, and
that all persons may use their recreations at such
meetings as before'."[1]

This return to the old conditions led twenty-five

[1] Neal: *History of the Puritans*, Vol. II, p. 213.

magistrates in Somerset to petition the King against the profaning of the Sunday by the holding of Wakes and Revels. They begged Charles to "grant us some more particular Declaration herein, That your Majesty's command concerning revels may not be thought to extend farther than to the upholding of civil feasting between neighbour and neighbour in their houses, and the orderly and seasonable use of manly exercises and activities which we all shall be most ready to maintain: And that we may have your Majesty's favour and allowance to suppress all the forementioned unlawful assemblies of church-ales, clerk-ales, and bid-ales and to punish all the forementioned disorders as heretofore we have done." [1]

Nothing was achieved by this petition and the re-issue by Charles of his father's Declaration of Sports made it clear that the King did not intend in any way to do anything which would seem to restrain the people from Sunday amusements. The petition however is valuable for our purpose as it shows, from the reference to the willingness of the petitioners to uphold "the orderly and seasonable use of manly exercises and activities" upon the Sunday, that it was not the expression of the wishes of extreme Puritans but of moderate, public-spirited men who saw in the licence and disorder which attended the Wakes and other Feasts fruitful sources of crime. This petition is in itself a sufficient answer to the letter sent by the Bishop of Bath and Wells to Laud.

These events in Somersetshire indicate very clearly the position which the authorities of the State Church had now taken up on the matter of Sunday amusements. So linked with the name Puritan was the doctrine of abstinence from anything upon the Sunday which would detract from the religious purpose of the day that those in the Anglican Church to whom the word was anathema were afraid to approve of any alteration

[1] Prynne: *Canterburies Doome*, p. 147.

in the mode, customary for so long, of spending the Sunday, lest they should be thought to be approving something Puritanical in origin. Perhaps no better example could be found than this of religious bigotry blinding men to the need for social reform, for there can be no doubt that the villages of Somerset would have been better places to live in, had the order of Richardson been allowed to continue, than they were when the lawlessness associated with some of the old church Feasts was liable at any time to break out.

On October 18th, 1633 Charles I re-issued the complete text of his father's Declaration of Sports adding to it the following statement: [1]

"Now out of a like pious care for the service of God, and for suppressing of any humours that oppose truth, and for the care, comfort and recreation of our well deserving people, We do ratify and publish this our blessed Father's Declaration: The rather because of late in some counties of our Kingdom, we find that under pretence of taking away abuses, there hath been a general forbidding, not only of ordinary meetings, but of the Feasts of the Dedication of the Churches, commonly called Wakes. Now our express will and pleasure is, that these Feasts with others shall be observed, and that our Justices of the Peace in their several divisions, shall look to it, both that all disorders there, may be prevented or punished, and that all neighbourhood and freedom, with manlike and lawful exercises be used. And we further command our Justices of Assizes in their several circuits, to see that no man do trouble or molest any of our loyal and dutiful people, in or for their lawful recreations, having first done their duty to God, and continuing in obedience to us and our laws. And of this command all our judges, justices of the peace, as well within as without, mayors, bailiffs,

[1] Gee and Hardy, pp. 528-532: Cox, *Literature of the Sabbath Question*, Vol. I, p. 444.

constables, and other officers, to take notice of, and
to see observed, as they tender Our displeasure. And
we further will, that publication of this our command
be made by order from the Bishops through all the
Parish Churches of their several Dioceses respectively."

The last sentence of the royal command was to
cause a great deal of trouble in the country. Whatever
might be the attitude of the Bishops themselves and
however their views might seem to receive the support
of many of their clergy, as in the case of the Bishop of
Bath and Wells already cited, there was a large body
of the ministers of the Anglican Church who were not
prepared to lend their authority to any attempt, even
though it were made by the King himself, to set the
clock back. Nearly a hundred years of Protestantism
had set their mark upon their clergy and laity alike of the
country and many there were who could not admit
that the citizens' "duty to God" could be as swiftly
discharged or easily forgotten as Charles seemed to think.

The degree to which the various bishops seem to have
enforced the reading of the Declaration varied con-
siderably. Thus the extent to which and the way in
which the royal command was published also varied.
Some, who disliked the tenor of the document but who
feared to disobey their diocesan, read it and then read
the fourth commandment, leaving, as it were, the
responsibility for either reconciling or choosing between
the two to the individual consciences of their hearers.
Many refused to read it and were suspended. William
Prynne, who drew up the charges made against Archbishop Laud in 1644 by the House of Commons, which
charges included the responsibility for the issue of this
Declaration by Charles I, says that hundreds of clergy
were suspended for not reading the order.[1] Fuller
says: "I hear the loudest, longest and thickest complaints come from the diocese of Norwich and of Bath

[1] Prynne: *Canterburies Doome*, p. 154.

and Wells." [1] The statement with regard to Bath and
Wells shows that the Bishop in his letter to Laud about
the suppression of Wakes and other festivals was only
quoting the opinion of a section of his clergy. Laud
himself seems to have suspended only three clergymen [2]
and in his defence to the charges brought against him
he said that most of those who were punished for not
reading the Declaration were punished by the Court of
High Commission and not by him personally. [3] He also
says that the Declaration was issued by the King's
special command and that there was no proof that he
had any responsibility for it. [4] Sir Edward Dering gives
examples of clergy who suffered for not reading the
Declaration. Thus the Chancellor of the diocese of
Winchester "confesseth he did suspend Mr. Bright, then
Vicar of Ebbesham, in Surrey, for not reading in the
church the King's Declaration for Sports." [5] In the
same way the Chancellor of the diocese of Rochester
confessed that he had suspended a Mr. Snelling and a
Mr. Pemberton for not reading the Book of Sports. [6]

Whether Laud or Charles himself should bear the
responsibility for the issue of the Declaration of 1633
is really a matter of indifference in the present connection. But there seems no reason to suppose that
Charles himself would require any urging on the part
of Laud to make the authoritative statement of a
position with which he had every sympathy. No doubt
Laud himself approved of the action of the monarch
because apart from anything else it was a blow at the
Puritans. The whole atmosphere of the Court however
was at this time an anti-Puritan one and that Charles
by his Declaration only desired for his people what he
and those surrounding him practised is shown by
Richard Baxter's account of the royal Court. He went

[1] *Fuller Church History*, Vol. III, p. 424.
[2] *Fuller III*, p. 425.
[3] Prynne, p. 505.
  Ditto, p. 504.
[5] *Proceedings in Kent*, p. 90.
[6] Ditto, pp. 92, 96.

to London in 1633 to obtain some knowledge of Court life under Sir Henry Herbert, the Master of the Revels, but he only stayed a month because, as he says: "I had quickly enough of the court. When I saw a stage-play instead of a sermon on the Lord's-days in the afternoon, and saw what course was there in fashion, and heard little preaching but what was as to one part against the Puritans, I was glad to be gone."[1]

Richard Baxter has left us a very vivid picture of the religious life of his home village about the end of the reign of James I and early in the reign of Charles I. Several passages are very well-known but even so they stand repetition and those that bear particularly on the matter of Sunday worship and Sunday observance will now be set down. Baxter was born in 1615 at Rowton in Shropshire and his father was a loyal Anglican who had no objections to the ceremonies of the State Church or to the authority of bishops, but who was yet dubbed a Puritan because he upheld a strict moral life as the ideal and because he believed in spending the Sunday in a devout fashion.

Baxter writes:[2] "We lived in a country that had but little preaching at all. In the village where I was born there was four readers successively in six years, ignorant men, and two of them immoral in their lives, who were all my schoolmasters. In the village where my father lived, there was a Reader of about eighty years of age that never preached, and had two churches about twenty miles distant. His eyesight failing him, he said Common Prayer without book: but for the reading of the Psalms and chapters, he got a common thresher and day labourer one year, and a taylor another year: (for the clerk could not read well) and at last he had a kinsman of his own (the excellentest stage-player in all the country, and a good gamester and a good fellow) that got Orders and supplied one of his places. After him

[1] *Autobiography of Richard Baxter*, edit. J. M. L. Thomas, p. 12.
[2] Ditto, pp. 3-4.

another younger kinsman, that could write and read, got Orders. And at the same time another neighbour's son that had been a while at school turned minister, and who would needs go further than the rest, ventured to preach (and after got a living in Staffordshire) and when he had been a preacher about twelve or sixteen years he was fain to give over, it being discovered that his Orders were forged by the first ingenious stage-player. After him another neighbour's son took Orders. When he had been a while an attorney's clerk, and a common drunkard, and tipled himself into so great poverty that he had no other to live; it was feared that he and more of them came by their Orders the same way with the forementioned person: These were the schoolmasters of my youth (except two of them) who read Common Prayer on Sundays and holy days, and taught school and tipled on the week-days, and whipped the boys when they were drunk, so that we changed them very oft. Within a few miles about us were near a dozen more ministers that were near eighty years old apiece, and never preached: poor ignorant readers, and most of them of scandalous lives. Only three or four constant competent preachers lived near us, and those (though conformable all save one) were the common marks of the people's obloquy and reproach, and any that had but gone to hear them, when he had no preaching at home, was made the derision of the vulgar rabble, under the odious name of Puritan."

Such a description, which needs no comment, shows why so many of the people welcomed Sunday games and why such Sunday games were often the scenes of disorder and drunkenness. Baxter adds to this account the following:[1] "In the village where I lived the reader read the Common Prayer briefly, and the rest of the day even till dark night almost, except eating time, was spent in dancing under a may-pole or a great tree not far from my father's door: where all the town did

[1] *Autobiography*, p. 6.

meet together. And though one of my father's own tenants was the piper, he could not restrain him, nor break the sport: so that we could not read the Scripture in our family without the great disturbance of the tabor and pipe and noise in the street! Many times my mind was inclined to be among them, and sometimes I broke loose from conscience and joined with them; and the more I did it the more I was inclined to it. But when I heard them call my father Puritan, it did much to cure me and alienate me from them: for I considered that my father's exercise of reading the Scripture, was better than theirs, and would surely be better thought on by all men at the last; and I considered what it was for that he and others were thus derided."

A picture such as Baxter paints makes one wonder at the attitude of mind which could imagine that instructions setting out the freedom of the people to do very much as they liked on the Sunday could do anything to improve the moral or religious tone of society in general. With these facts in mind one ceases to wonder that some Puritans were led to set extremely strict limits to what was permissible upon the Sunday. Desperate situations need drastic remedies. What the Puritans realized, and what the King and the bishops were strangely blind to, is well expressed by Fuller when he writes: "Many complain that man's badness took occasion to be worse, under the protection of these sports permitted unto them. For, although liberty on the Lord's day may be so limited in the notions of learned men, as to make it lawful, it is difficult (if not impossible) so to confine it in the actions of lewd people but that their liberty will degenerate into licentiousness." [1] The whole history of the Sunday in this country since Reformation times was proof of Fuller's perspicacity. The Puritan theory about the Sunday might be built, in many cases, upon a false or semi-false foundation but it was a theory which, translated into

[1] Fuller: *Church History III*, p. 425.

action, was what was needed for the social improvement of the people. The theory of the State Church on the other hand, while it read very beautifully as set out in the early Reformation documents, had been on trial for nearly a century and was no nearer, but probably farther from, translation into practice in the reign of Charles I than it had been early in Elizabeth's reign.

Charles I's Declaration of 1633 naturally provided a useful excuse for those people, whether dignitaries of the Church or laymen, who wished to attack those of the clergy who held strict views on the Sunday question. Mention has already been made of the way many were deprived for not reading the Declaration but there were other cases where men got into trouble because they felt it necessary in no measured terms to denounce the document and not merely ignore it. For example, the churchwardens, sidesmen and some ten parishioners of the church at Shaftesbury in Dorset presented their minister, Edward Williams, in 1634 for certain irregularities in the conduct of worship but especially for preaching against the Declaration "in a most high kind of terrification as if it were a most dreadful thing and near damnable, if not absolutely damnable, to use any recreations on the Sabbath or Lord's Day." [1]

Similar dissatisfaction to that expressed by Fuller shows amongst others who did not find in the Parish Church all the spiritual comfort that they required. A certain William Dodson of Rothwell in Northamptonshire, a mercer, was brought before the Ecclesiastical Commissioners for various reasons and in his examination admitted to having religious exercises including the repetition of sermons in his own home on Sunday afternoons, such devotions being restricted to his own family however. He definitely expressed his opinion that Sunday sports were unlawful and that two sermons each Sunday were a necessity for salvation and that it

[1] *Cal. State Papers Domestic*, Vol. CCLXVII No. 6.

was therefore permissible for a man to leave his own Parish Church for some other if thereby he might hear a sermon when he would otherwise not do so. [1]

A letter of Dr. John Andrews, a clergyman in the diocese of Lincoln, to the Chancellor of Lincoln, in 1634, reveals the attitude of mind of those who tried to blame the Puritans for causing irregularities in a parish. He says his views are not acceptable to the bulk of the clergy and laity of the district because they are inclined to puritanism and he is not, and he charges the people of his parish with, amongst other things, travelling on Sundays to other parishes to hear puritanical sermons and irreverent conduct during service in that many sit in the service with their hats on, lie along the pews, and will not kneel during prayer. [2] One is tempted to conclude that, dissatisfied with his slackness, the more deeply religious of his parishioners had sought spiritual comfort elsewhere while the more irreligious had taken advantage of the doctor's indifference to do just as they liked. Puritanism was a challenge to such men in that it set a higher standard of personal conduct for clergy and laity alike than was customary.

Laud, when defending himself against the charge of responsibility for the issue of the Declaration of Sports, said that that issue was occasioned in part by the publication in 1632 of a book by T. Brabourne in support of the strict observance of Sunday. [3] This is a reminder that a regular battle of pens was in progress at the time between the opposing camps on the Sunday question. It is questionable whether either side gained from a great deal of what was written which was of too partisan a nature to do more than inflame tempers and harden prejudices. The bulk of the books written on the matter have long since fallen into oblivion and are not even useful for the present purpose of trying to re-construct

[1] *Cal. State Papers Domestic*, Vol. CCLXVII No. 90.
[2] *Cal. State Papers Domestic*, Vol. CCLXIX No. 36.
[3] Prynne: *Canterburies Doome*, p. 504.

a picture of the period because they are mere wordy arguments based upon usages of Scripture or the Ancient Fathers of the Church and entirely remote from the problem of the seventeenth century. But there are certain exceptions and it will be well to glance at some of these at this point.

In 1634 there appeared an edition in English of a book first published in Latin in 1622 by Dr. Prideaux, Bishop of Worcester. This expresses very moderately the orthodox Anglican position on *The Doctrine of the Sabbath* which was the title of the book. In it he sets out the duties of the Christian upon the Sunday on the lines of the King's Book of 1543. He will have nothing to do with any attempt to bind the Christian by the Jewish law or custom and says: "we only are so far to abstain from work, as it is an impediment to the performance of such duties as are then commanded." [1] No doubt the true Christian in Prideaux's estimation would be so occupied with his devotions or charitable works that he would have no time for mundane affairs except those of necessity. But in the imperfect world of the seventeenth century all were not true Christians and would find a lot of time for works that were far from necessary under the cloak of this theory. Prideaux would allow, under "works of charity", recreations "Which serve lawfully to refresh our spirits, and nourish mutual neighbourhood among us." [2] Unfortunately as we have seen too many desired to pass the time by refreshing themselves in the alehouses or in quarrelling with their neighbours.

In 1636 Peter Heylyn brought out his *History of the Sabbath* in which he supported the doctrine of the State Church and endeavoured to trace out the history of Sunday observance up to his own day. Several references have already been made to this book and it contains a lot of information which is of considerable

[1] Prideaux: *Doctrine of the Sabbath*, p. 38.
[2] Prideaux, p. 39.

value to the historian of the Sunday question up to
Heylyn's own time. On the other hand, in face of all
the facts which we have already had under review, one
is amazed that Heylyn, in his dedication which is
addressed to Charles I, can write thus: "In such a
Church as this, so settled in a constant practice of
Religious Offices and so confirmed by godly Canons, for
the performance of the same, there was no fear, that
ever the Lord's Day (the Day appointed by God's
Church for his public service) would have been over-
run by the profane neglect of any pious duties on that
day required."[1] The author must surely have been too
busy tracing out the history of the past to observe what
was going on around him in his own day. It is not surprising, particularly after the above quotation, to find
that Heylyn blames those who have sought to overthrow the doctrine of the Church by Jewish "super-
stitions", and that he applauds the issue by Charles of
the Declaration of Sports. Heylyn's purpose in writing
is to awaken "those men who have so long dreamt of a
Sabbath day, that now they will not be persuaded that
it is a dream."[2]

One passage, in which Heylyn claims to give his own
experience of the extreme supporters of this "dream",
is deserving of attention. No doubt it is biassed, though
no more so than some of the statements made in books
written upon the other side of the controversy, but
allowing for that it gives some idea of the extremes to
which some of the least wise amongst the Sabbatarians
went. This is Heylyn's experience:[3]

"Some I have known (for in this point I will say
nothing without good assurance) who in a furious kind
of zeal have run into the open streets, yea, and searched
private houses too, to look for such as spent those
hours, on the Lord's day, in lawful pastimes, which

[1] Heylyn: *History of the Sabbath*, Book I, Dedication.
[2] Ditto.
[3] Heylyn: *History of the Sabbath*, Book II, pp. 255-256.

were not destinate, by the Church, to God's public service: and having found them out scattered the Company, brake the instruments: and, if my memory fail me not, the musician's head too: and, which is more they thought that they were bound in conscience so to do. Others, that will not suffer either baked or roast to be made ready for their dinners, on their Sabbath day, lest by so doing, they should eat and drink to their own damnation, according to the doctrine preached unto them. Some that upon the Sabbath will not sell a pint of wine, or the like commodity: though wine was made by God, not only for man's often infirmities, but to make glad his heart, and refresh his spirits; and therefore no less required on the Lord's day than on any other.

"Others, which have refused to carry provender to an house on the supposed Sabbath day: though our Redeemer thought it no impiety on the true Sabbath day indeed to lead poor cattle to the water . . . So for the female sex; maid-servants I have met with, some two or three, who though they were content to dress their meat upon the Sabbath; yet by no means would be persuaded either to wash their dishes or make clean their kitchen. But that which most of all affects me is that a gentlewoman at whose house I lay in Leicester, the last Northern Progress Anno 1634 expressed a great desire to see the King and Queen who were then both there. And when I proffered her my service, to satisfy that loyal longing, she thanked me but refused the favour because it was the Sabbath day."

While one is inclined to smile at the refusal of some of these people to cook a meal or perform some other necessary household task on Sunday one is forced to see that Heylyn's attitude reveals the dangers of permitting unnecessary Sunday labour. One feels that in his desire to enjoy himself upon the Sunday Heylyn might not scruple to cause others to do a great deal of work which would make the day far from being one of rest or enjoyment for them.

Dr. Robert Sanderson, Bishop of Lincoln, published in 1636 *The Case of the Sabbath* which was another reasonable book in support of the Anglican position. He accepted the Declaration of 1633 as settling the matter of the lawfulness of Sunday sports but he pleaded for a moderate use of such sports. One or two of his observations on the matter of Sunday recreations are worth noticing as for example his statement that: "walking and discoursing, with men of liberal education, is a pleasant recreation: it is no way delightsome to the ruder sort of people, who scarce account anything a sport which is not loud and boisterous."[1] This distinction has not entirely disappeared to-day with all our twentieth century education and yet it is one which those who consider the problem to-day are as prone to ignore as were almost all the people who debated the matter in the seventeenth century. Yet while Sanderson deserves credit for pointing out this fact he does not make it clear how the "ruder sort of people" are to be trained to a higher standard. Perhaps he did not imagine such a training possible and therefore would allow them the sport they enjoyed even though it were "loud and boisterous." Unfortunately it not only was that, in itself a source of nuisance to more devoutly-minded people, but was often criminal and dangerous, and neither the State Church nor the State itself should have felt complacent under a system which had such unfortunate possibilities.

Sanderson further states that sports and recreation should be used in moderation and that "they be so used, as that they may rather make men the fitter for God's service the rest of the day, and for the works of their vocations the rest of the week, than any way

[1] *Works of Robert Sanderson*, Vol. V, p. 15.

hinder and disable them thereunto, by over-wearying the body, or immoderately affecting the mind."[1] A fine ideal once again, but surely one that the "ruder sort of people" would hardly appreciate or be able to attain and yet they were the people to whom it must chiefly apply if Sunday recreations were to be a source of good rather than of harm.

The reasonableness and welcome absence of bitterness in Sanderson's book is shown in the passage which says that people must not use Sunday sports doubtingly and that if an individual is not satisfied in his own mind of the lawfulness of such sports he ought not to use them. People, says the writer, should "be severer towards themselves than towards other men in the use of their Christian liberty herein not making their own opinion or practice a rule to their brethren."[2] But while one admires the spirit of Sanderson's book one cannot help seeing that its writer was entirely aloof from the practical issues of his own day. The Protestant Church of England had had nearly a century in which to try to educate the people of the country to appreciate the view which Sanderson expresses and which was in its essentials the view of that Church and many of the people were no nearer understanding or accepting it than they had been at the beginning. On the other hand many people had been forced by circumstances to take up a new position as to the obligations of the Sunday and so convinced were a number of these people of the correctness of their unorthodox views that they would not be content unless they could bring, by force if persuasion failed, others to share it.

It is quite a contrast in spirit and in point of view to turn from Sanderson to William Prynne. In 1633 had appeared his Histriomastix or Players' Scourge in which he had severely attacked amusements in general. The Star Chamber punished him for issuing this book

[1] *Works of Sanderson*, Vol. V, p. 16.
[2] Ditto.

by a £5,000 fine, the pillory and the cutting off of his ears. In passing it is well perhaps to remind ourselves of sentences like these because they not only illustrate the conviction of those who were willing to endure such punishments rather than keep silence on what they believed to be the truth, but they also help us to understand the strain of austerity and fanaticism in the Puritans who were made to suffer in this way.

In the Histriomastix Prynne particularly condemns dancing and stage-plays upon the Sunday and after quoting a law promulgated by some of the Christian Emperors against Sunday amusements says: "O that this godly law were now in force with Christians! Then plays and pastimes on Lord's-day evenings would not be so frequent; then those who had served God at prayers and sermons in the daytime would not so seriously serve the world, the flesh, the devil, in dancing, dicing, masques, and stage plays in the night, beginning perchance the Lord's day (like the foolish Galatians) in the spirit but ending it in the flesh, as alas too many carnal Christians do."[1] Undoubtedly the fact that Prynne in this book indiscriminately attacked almost all forms of amusement, wherever participated in, weakened his strictures upon Sunday amusements. On the other hand it has been surmised that Prynne, and others amongst the Puritans who united with him to condemn all amusements at all times, had been led to adopt this attitude partly because Sunday was the usual day, and for many people the only day, upon which amusements could be enjoyed. Thus the two were so closely associated that the clearest course to adopt seemed to be that of banning all amusements and leaving people with six days in which to give themselves wholeheartedly to their secular toil and one day which was to be devoted entirely to God's service and meditation upon God's purposes.

A more apposite book in the present connection and

[1] Prynne: *Histriomastix*, p. 470.

one less well known than the *Histriomastix* was Prynne's volume published in 1636 under the title *A Divine Tragedy lately Acted* or "A collection of sundry memorable examples of God's judgments upon Sabbath breakers." In this curious book Prynne gives fifty-five examples of instances where, in his belief, God has punished people for breaking the Sabbath since the publication of the royal Declaration two years previously. In his artless introduction the author says with regard to these examples "for the truth of them I have good testimony under the hands of men of sufficient credit for the most of them; and the rest hath come to our ears by credible report. If it shall to fall out that one or two or so should prove otherwise either for the substance or circumstance, let not the reader blame me."[1]

While not feeling it incumbent to interpret the accidents as blows of Divine displeasure, and while remembering that a few may be untrue, the modern reader will find from a cursory study of the book more evidence that Sunday sports were quite common if he still requires such evidence. There was bowling in Dorsetshire—a thing illegal as we have seen and not made permissible—Morris dancing and Whitsun Ales in Worcestershire: football on the ice near Gainsborough: youths playing Cat in London: ordinary football at Colchester: and many a similar occurrence. The injury, damage and disorder that resulted from some of these sports show why it was that many reasonable citizens did not desire them even if they did not all share the view which Prynne had of them.

This book of Prynne's was naturally not regarded with any favour by the High Church party. Every effort was made to suppress it and copies had to be circulated secretly. Thus we get a document endorsed by Laud's Secretary giving an account of the examination before the Bishop of Bath and Wells of the

[1] Prynne: *A Divine Tragedy*, p. 3.

clerk and vicar and others of Dowltinge in Somerset regarding the distribution of *The Divine Tragedy* in the county. From this it seems that the copies in question were traced to a certain John Ash of Freshford, a clothier, who had received two hundred sent anonymously from London with instructions to sell them at 8d. each and to send the money to a minister named Burton in London.[1] When the Puritan writers had to work under the dangers and difficulties that beset Prynne it is not surprising that fewer of their works worthy of notice on the question of Sunday observance are available than those written by their opponents.

Before leaving this subject of the books published at this stage of the controversy one other will be noticed. In 1636 there appeared *A Treatise of the Sabbath* which it was explained was "written in French by David Primerose B.D. . . . minister of the gospel in the Protestant Church of Rouen, Englished . . . by his father G.P.D.D." The writer's opinion can be seen from the following sentences. "If divine service be publicly practised before and after noon in the Church, whereof he is a member, he must not soothe himself with a fond opinion, that he hath done his duty when he hath been present at either of them, and forsaken one of the two, to bestow it on some other thing. That time ordained by the Church being expired, and the whole service of that day finished, when he is come home, and is alone, he is free to do what he will, so it be honest and lawful; to work, or to refresh himself, for in that he sinneth not against God and transgresseth not His Commandments. If he will pass the rest of the day in actions of religion he shall do well; if he will spend it on other ordinary and common actions of this life, he shall not do ill."[2] Once again while the theory might be admirable there was too much loophole for abuse, particularly in the possibility of Sunday labour. It will be seen that

[1] *Third Report of the Historical MSS. Commission* 1872, p. 191.
[2] Primerose: *A Treatise of the Sabbath*, p. 307.

almost all the writers who support the attitude of the
State Church leave so much to the individual judgment
the matter of Sunday labour. That is one of the great
weaknesses from the social point of view of their theory.
The individual could not be trusted to decide for himself
whether he should or should not work upon the Sunday.
The result of his decision had too great a bearing upon
the well-being of the community as a whole for that to
be allowed satisfactorily.

It seems strange that the State Church, which under
Laud was claiming peculiar autocratic powers, should
have been content in this one particular to leave the
individual free to please himself and order his own
conduct. The explanation of course lies in the fact that
to attempt to issue stricter regulations for the observance of Sunday in any particular was to admit the truth
of one of the Puritan doctrines and that was the last
thing that the extreme clerical party desired to do. That
this was so was unfortunate because the seventeenth
century was the century in which the shopkeeper and
craftsmen and labourer were particularly free from
supervision and control. The rules of the craft guild
in the Middle Ages would have seen to it that Sunday
work was not done but these associations had entirely
passed away as far as effective control of industry was
concerned and the regulations of Elizabeth's reign only
covered matters like wages and apprenticeship and not
the actual hours permissible for work. Thus, as we
have seen, the Stuart craftsman or shopkeeper was
inclined in certain cases to follow his trade or open his
shop on the Sunday and the State and the State Church
seemed inclined to leave it to him to do so if he wished.
Had this state of affairs been allowed to continue, many
people would before long have found themselves working for at any rate six and a half days of the week and
no doubt in many cases seven days, for the inability of
the Church to enforce even its minimum requirements
was being exemplified more and more.

That conditions did not grow more lax than they did and that some check was left upon abuses on the Sunday during the period when Charles I, with the advice of Strafford and Laud, ruled very much as he pleased is due to the zeal and example of those whose standard for the keeping of Sunday was higher than the official one. Not only the persuasion of those preachers whom Laud would have dubbed Puritan, even though they had no quarrel with the regulations of the Church to which they still belonged, together with those who had left the Church, but the regard for decency and good order among many of the magistrates, who were becoming more and more Puritan in their views, secured a day of rest and quietude in many places. Such a magistrate was Sir Robert Harley whose care to preserve the sacredness of the day made him enemies amongst those who desired to work upon it, as for example in 1639 when a man brought a lawsuit against him because, as Lady Harley thought, Sir Robert "made him pay for his horse that carried a load on the Sabbath."[1]

In the tribute paid to Sir Robert Harley at his funeral was included this passage:— "Among other things, how would he vindicate the Sabbath from contempt! Profaneness durst not appear upon the face of it. By this means the congregations were frequented on the Lord's days and many thousand souls, prevented from their sinful sports, sat under the droppings of the word. He paid a dear devotion of love to the Lord's day (that pearl of the week). When the licentious sinfulness ofttimes cried it down, how often have I heard him plead it up with excellency of arguments! . . . He rejoiced still when the Sabbath came, and was usually more cheerful that day than others, even in his sickness."[2]

The example and influence of such a man, although perhaps over strict at times for some, did more to better

[1] *Letters of Lady Brilliana Harley, p. 61.*
[2] Ditto, pp. 15-16.

the social condition of the country than all the books of men like Sanderson or Primerose could ever hope to do.

CHAPTER X

LEGISLATIVE EFFORTS 1640-1660

FOR the eleven years during which no Parliament had met there had been little or no opportunity for public opinion on the matter of the observance of Sunday to make itself felt. The Long Parliament which first met towards the end of 1640 was plunged at once into a welter of political business which might have been expected to leave it no time for other affairs. Yet as early as the following May the House of Commons could find time for the reading of a Bill forbidding bargemen or lightermen from loading or unloading goods on the Sunday.[1] By the end of the year the Bill had reached the House of Lords but it failed to get beyond the Committee stage.[2]

While the Bill was still under consideration an incident occurred which clearly showed the attitude of Parliament towards Sunday work. It was necessary on Sunday, August 8th, 1641 for Parliament to meet to transact urgent business before the departure of Charles I for Scotland the next day. As we have noticed it was no uncommon thing in the reigns of Elizabeth and the Stuart kings for the Council to transact business on Sunday. Parliament never seems to have met on Sunday but then before 1640 Parliament was rarely concerned in any matter of urgency because it was not powerful enough to demand to be consulted upon such affairs. Now however that the necessity arose for a Sunday sitting Parliament felt that it must justify its

[1] Rushworth: *Historical Collections*. Third Part (Vol. I), p. 277.
[2] *Lords' Journals IV*, pp. 488 and 514.

action in so doing. The House of Commons assembled at 6 a.m., listened to a sermon, and began their business at 9 a.m. with the resolution to discuss nothing beyond matters immediately concerning the advancement of religion and the safety of the country. It and the House of Lords published the following declaration in justification of their conduct:—[1]

"Whereas both Houses of Parliament found it fit to sit upon the 8th day of August, being the Lord's Day, for many urgent and unexpected occasions, concerning the safety of the kingdom, they being so straitened in time, by reason of His Majesty's resolution to begin his journey towards Scotland on Monday following, early in the morning; that it was not otherwise possible for to settle and order the affairs of the Kingdom, either for the Government thereof in the King's absence, or for the present safety as was requisite upon the present necessities; though the Houses thought it necessary to sit, yet the Lords and Commons now assembled in Parliament think it meet to declare, that they would not have done this, but upon inevitable necessity; the peace and safety both of Church and State being so deeply concerned: which they do hereby declare, to the end, that neither any other inferior court or council, or any other person, may draw this into example, or make use of it for their encouragement, in neglecting the due observation of the Lord's Day."

That a House of Commons, composed as this one was at this time of "Puritans and moderate Episcopalians, of Roundheads and constitutional Cavaliers acting in union,"[2] and the House of Lords felt it necessary to publish such a declaration is indicative of the degree to which public opinion on the matter of Sunday observance had changed. This was not the utterance of a

---

[1] Rushworth Third Part (Vol. I), p. 362: *Tudor and Stuart Proclamations*, p. 229.
[2] G. M. Trevelyan: *History of England*, p. 403.

narrow sect or of a clamant minority but the measured statement of two responsible bodies, one, at any rate, of which was closely in touch with the different currents of thought flowing through the land.

A month later, on September 8th, the House of Commons made its attitude on this question still clearer by issuing a resolution to the effect "That the Lord's Day shall be duly observed and sanctified; all dancing or other sports, either before or after divine service, be forborne and restrained, and that the preaching of God's word be permitted in the afternoon in the several churches and chapels of the Kingdom; and that ministers and preachers be encouraged thereunto."[1] The House of Commons sent this, together with other resolutions on Church ceremonies and customs, to the House of Lords for their concurrence but the House of Lords returned no answer, possibly because they did not agree to some of the other points raised or possibly because they were unwilling to commit themselves to such a definite condemnation of all Sunday amusements.

Thus, fairly early in the life of the Long Parliament, the House of Commons, which could not as yet be termed predominantly Puritan, except in the widest and best sense of that term, including in it faithful supporters of the State Church as well as dissenters from its rules, made it quite clear that Sunday was a day to be kept free from all business, except in cases of extreme necessity, and from mundane pleasures. In taking this attitude they undoubtedly interpreted correctly the mind of the majority of the responsible and reverent sections of society. That they did not represent the wishes of an irresponsible and thoughtless element, possibly a fairly large element, is also true. This was because this element had not as yet been sufficiently educated in the principles which lay behind the attitude of those who desired a more reverent Sunday. The House of Commons realized this and hence it not

[1] Gee and Hardy, p. 552. *Journals of Commons II*, p. 279.

only took steps, as suggested in the order of September 8th, to encourage preaching but it found it necessary in the succeeding years to pass a number of Ordinances which aimed at restraining those who would not, of their own free will, observe the Sunday in a religious manner.

In February 1643 an Ordinance was issued which exhorted the people to repent of their national sins among which was placed the "wicked profanation of the Lord's Day, by sports and gamings, formerly encouraged even by Authority."[1] This was followed in the next month by a request to the Lord Mayor of London asking him to enforce the statutes for the proper observance of the Sunday. The Lord Mayor thereupon gave orders to all responsible officials not to permit[2] "any person or persons, in time of divine service, or at any time on the Lord's Day, to be tippling in any tavern, inn, tobacco-shop, alehouse, or other victualling-house whatsoever; nor suffer any fruiterers or herb women to stand with fruit, herbs or other victuals or wares, in any streets, lanes, or alleys . . . or any other ways to put those or any other things to sale, on that day at any time of the day, or in the evening thereof; or any milk-women to cry milk . . . nor to permit or suffer any person or persons to use or exercise upon that day their labour in unloading any vessels of fruit or other goods, and carrying goods on shore or in the streets or to do any unlawful exercises or pastimes." Innkeepers might receive ordinary guests or travellers but nobody else.

This order is valuable because it seems to show that, as has been noticed before, the people whom those in authority thought it necessary to proceed against were those especially whose conduct on the Sunday was not merely irreligious but calculated to prove a definite annoyance to those who desired a quiet, orderly Sun-

[1] *Acts and Ordinances of the Interregnum*, edit. Firth and Rait, Vol. I, p. 81.
[2] Ed. Husband: *A Collection of Ordinances*, p. 7.

day. The law had apparently succeeded in suppressing the noisy butcher but his place had been taken by street-seller of fruit and other things. In the narrow streets of London—old London before the replanning and widening that followed the Fire—any street-sellers would be a nuisance to those who wished to proceed quietly to and from Divine Service while the shouting of their wares by such vendors would be an offence to all who wished for a little respite from the toil of the other days of the week. Those who haunted the taverns and similar places were, as we have seen, notoriously those who shirked the obligatory Church-going and those who were most likely to be the cause of any riot or disturbance. Primarily then this order would secure a quieter, more restful Sunday and therein would advantage all, including those who were by it forbidden to work upon this one day of the week.

Both the House of Commons and the House of Lords seem to have felt that, in spite of the existing laws and instructions, the people of the country were in need of more positive direction upon the matter of Sunday observance. That this should be so is not surprising seeing the difference of opinion which had existed between King and Parliament on the matter, between different groups in the State Church, and between different authors. To clear the position up the two Houses issued another Ordinance on the 8th of April 1644 in the following terms: [1]

"Forasmuch as the Lord's Day, notwithstanding several good laws heretofore made, hath been not only greatly profaned but divers ungodly books have been published by the prelatical faction against the morality of that day, and to countenance the profanation of the same, to the manifest indangering of souls, prejudice of the true religion, great dishonour of Almighty God, and provocation of his just wrath and indignation against the Land.

[1] *Acts and Ordinances*, Vol. I, pp. 420-421.

"The Lords and Commons for remedy thereof, do order and ordain . . . That all the laws enacted and in force, concerning the observation of the Lord's-day be carefully put in execution; and that all and singular person or persons whatsoever, shall in every Lord's day apply themselves to the sanctification of the same, by exercising themselves thereon, in the duties of piety and true religion, publicly and privately: and that no person or persons whatsoever shall publicly cry, shew forth, or expose to sale, any wares, merchandises, fruit, herbs, goods or chattels whatsoever, upon the Lord's day, or any part thereof; upon pain, That every person so offending, shall forfeit the same goods so cried, shewed forth, or put to sale: and that no person or persons whatsoever shall, without reasonable cause for the same, travel, carry burdens, or do any worldly labours, or work whatsoever, on that day, or any part thereof". The penalties for the latter offences were ten shillings for travelling and five shillings for carrying a burden or working.

The Ordinance continued to enact: "That no person or persons shall hereafter upon the Lord's Day use, exercise, keep, maintain, or be present at any wrestlings, shootings, bowling, ringing of bells for pleasure or pastime, masque, wake, otherwise called feasts, Church-ale, dancing, games, sport or pastime whatsoever." The penalty here was a five shilling fine for all over fourteen years of age.

If any children of the or under the age of fourteen broke any of the regulations the parents or guardians or tutors responsible for them were fined twelvepence.

Then came the following clause: "And because the profanation of the Lord's-day hath been heretofore greatly occasioned by May-poles (a heathenish vanity, generally abused to superstition and wickedness) the Lords and Commons do further order and ordain That all and singular May-poles that are, or shall be erected, shall be taken down and removed. . . . It is further ordained . . . that the King's Declaration concerning observing of Wakes, and use of exercise and recreation upon the Lord's Day; the Book entitled 'The King's Majesty's Declaration to his subjects concerning lawful Sports to be used'; and all other books and pamphlets that have been or shall be written, printed or published, against the morality of the fourth commandment, or of the Lord's Day, or to countenance the profanation thereof, be called in, seized, suppressed and publicly burnt. . . . Provided and be it Declared That nothing in this Ordinance shall extend to the prohibiting of dressing of meat in private families, or the dressing and sale of victuals in a moderate way in inns or victualling-houses for the use of such as cannot otherwise be provided for; or to the crying or selling milk" before 9 a.m. and after 4 p.m. from September 10th to March 10th or before 8 a.m. or after 5 p.m. for the rest of the year.

Finally the Ordinance said: "Whereas there is great breach of the Sabbath by rogues, vagabonds, and beggars, it is further Ordained That the Lord Mayor of the City of London, and all Justices of the Peace . . . shall . . . cause all laws against rogues and vagabonds and beggars to be put in due execution; and take order that all rogues, vagabonds, and beggars do on every Sabbath day repair to some Church and chapel, and remain there soberly and orderly during the time of Divine-Worship."

So much space has been given to this Ordinance because it so clearly represents the position taken up by both Houses of Parliament now that the Civil War had begun and Parliament had lost those members who supported the High Church view. The Ordinance is in line with the progressive development of Parliamentary thought over half a century and more. It does not denote any revolution of theory. It simply shows that, with the removal of the King's authority, and the withdrawal of that minority who continued to hold to the view that Sunday was a fitting day for sport and amusement and even work, provided the obligations of worship had been discharged, the bulk of the members of the legislative body were able to give expression, more completely than hitherto, to their belief that Sunday was a day to be marked not only by worship but by the absence of ordinary work and pleasures.

Since the end of the previous century as we have seen those who desired a more sober Sunday had been forced to base their claim upon the unchanging authority of the Fourth Commandment. This fact is now embodied in this Ordinance. The suspicion which all Protestants, with the exception of the High Church party of the State Church, had of anything savouring of Roman Catholic and pagan practices (the two were almost inseparably connected in the minds of most people) is revealed in the reference to May-poles which were also bound to come in for censure because it was customary to carry out the celebrations connected with them on the Sunday. The curious objection to bell-ringing which appears constantly in the regulations of this period can be partly accounted for on the same lines. It is quite clear that some people found as much enjoyment in bell-ringing as in other sports and amusements and therefore it seemed only logical to prohibit the practice which in such cases was in no sense a necessary work or a devotional exercise and which might disturb the calm of those who wished to use the day for quiet meditation.

That the Ordinance condemned the King's Declaration to be burnt is not at all surprising. It was simply doing what, at the time of its issue, many thoughtful people would have liked to have done. Probably none but the High Church party and the more irresponsible elements in the country had ever approved it and now was a fitting opportunity to make this fact clear.

Remembering the attitude which those who advocated a free-and-easy Sunday had adopted while the power rested in their hands and remembering also the gloomy picture which they had painted of the ideals of their opponents, we might be surprised to find this Ordinance so very moderate in tone did we not remember, as has been already mentioned, that it was the logical sequence of a long period of legislation and attempted legislation. After all the Ordinance really did no more than attempt to enforce the type of Sunday which could be said to have been implied in the early regulations of the post-Reformation Church of England. A day filled with meditation, public and private devotions, and sick-visiting would leave no room for ordinary work or games. If the High Church party had considered that the vagueness of the early regulations left scope for a freedom of interpretation which would permit such things the Puritan party had at least equal right to place their own interpretation upon them. Time had shown that people abused the liberty of the day, if left to themselves, both by work and by their conduct at their sports and amusements and to many it seemed that only the discipline of prohibition would effect a cure.

Some may consider the ban upon travelling harsh. Yet in the light of seventeenth century conditions it is not so. Few had any need to travel upon the Sunday. Even the King's Declaration had forbidden people to leave their own parish for sports elsewhere. If work and sport were not permissible there would be very few under any necessity to leave their own village. It must be remembered that very few people had friends or acquaintances anywhere but in their own parish in those days and most people if they travelled would have to do so on foot so that they would be almost bound to miss attending the services in their own Parish Church which all parties were agreed upon as a necessity.

Lastly it must be observed that the Ordinance does not attempt to impose any restriction upon the ordinary domestic work necessary for the health and comfort of

all. This needs pointing out because there were those
amongst the minority of ultra-fanatical Puritans who
tried to impose irksome and unnecessary regulations.
But of such there is no trace in this Ordinance.

Had Parliament been content to leave the matter of
Sunday observance where the Ordinance of 1644 placed
it its action would have been commendable on the
ground of the necessity of removing existing abuses and
protecting those who did not wish to work on Sunday.
Unfortunately it was not so content. Those of its
members who had become soaked in the deep, if narrow,
religious teaching which had its fount in the Old Testament sincerely believed that it was their duty to train
all their fellow-citizens to enjoy the same wells of
inspiration. In one sense this is to their credit. Their
religion prompted them to positive action and not to a
mere static negativism. This is a point on which they
have frequently been misjudged and misrepresented as
if a "thou shalt not" was the beginning and end of their
teaching. Having prohibited certain things they did
try to substitute a desire for something which they
regarded as infinitely better. That they did so often by
compulsory efforts was but natural in the age in which
they lived when compulsion played a very large part
in any educative system. This tendency is illustrated
by an Ordinance which was issued in 1645 which aimed
at compelling people not merely to abstain from what
was considered wrong upon the Sunday but to practise
what was regarded as right. It will be well therefore to
consider those clauses of this Ordinance which bring
out this point, not because they would be likely to seem
presumptive or impossible of achievement in their own
day, as they appear in ours, but because they mark a
fresh step in the story of the course of events connected
with the story which we are trying to trace.

An Ordinance of the 4th of January 1645, for the purpose of substituting a new Directory for the public
worship of God in place of the old Book of Common

Prayer, had the following directions in it with reference
to the sanctification of Sunday:[1]

"The Lord's day ought to be so remembered before
hand, as that all worldly business of our ordinary
callings may be so ordered, and so timely and seasonably laid aside, as they may not be impediments to the
due sanctifying of the Day when it comes.

"The whole Day is to be celebrated as holy to the
Lord, both in public and private, as being the Christian
Sabbath. To which end it is requisite, that there be a
holy cessation or resting all the Day from all unnecessary labours, and an abstaining, not only from all
sports and pastimes, but also from all worldly words and
thoughts.

"That the diet on the Day be so ordered, as that
neither servants be unnecessarily detained from the
public worship of God, nor any other persons hindered
from the sanctifying that Day.

"That there be private preparation of every person
and family, by prayer for themselves, and for God's
assistance of the Minister, and for a blessing upon his
ministry, and by such other holy exercises as may
further dispose them to a more comfortable communion with God in his public ordinances.

"That all the people meet so timely for public worship
that the whole Congregation may be present at the
beginning, and with one heart solemnly join together
in all parts of the public Worship; and not depart till
after the Blessing.

"That what time is vacant between or after the solemn
meetings of the Congregation in public be spent in
Reading, Meditation, Repetition of Sermons (especially
by calling their families to an account of what they have
heard) and catechizing of them, holy conferences,
prayer for a blessing upon the Public Ordinances, saying of Psalms, visiting the sick, relieving the poor, and

[1] *Acts and Ordinances*, Vol. I, pp. 598-599.

such like duties of piety, charity and mercy, accounting the Sabbath a delight."

As a Church document setting forth an ideal for the members of such a community to aim at the Ordinance would be admirable. That it was put forward as a State command shows the liability to weakness of any system where religious fervour tends to usurp the functions of Impartial State-craft. It was reasonable and possible for the State to prohibit Sunday labour and equally possible and, at any rate at that time on account of the abuses attendant upon the custom, justifiable for the State to ban Sunday amusements, but it was neither rational nor possible to attempt to order a man's thoughts or his private devotions. Yet because the Puritans attempted to do the latter we should not allow this to blind us, as has so often happened, to the very great social benefit that they did in achieving the former, thereby crowning the work that many true citizens both within and without the State Church had had in view for many decades.

It was not to be expected that Parliament would achieve immediately all that it set out to do by these laws and ordinances concerning the observance of Sunday. People who had been inclined to disregard any exhortation to keep the day holy in the past and who had been fortified in their determination to amuse themselves as they pleased upon, at any rate, part of the day by two royal declarations permitting such conduct were unlikely easily to forgo such enjoyments. Consequently in October 1645 Parliament authorized the suspension from the Sacrament of the Lord's Supper of "Any person that shall upon the Lord's Day use any dancing, playing at dice, or cards, or any other game, masking, wake, shooting, bowling, playing at football or stool-ball, wrestling, or that shall make, or resort unto any plays, interludes, fencing, bull-baiting or bear-baiting, or that shall use hawking, hunting, or coursing, fishing, or fowling, or that shall publicly expose any wares to sale, otherwise than as is provided by an Ordinance of Parliament of the 6th April, 1644. Any person that shall travel on the Lord's Day without reasonable cause."[1]

The Puritans usually have to bear heavy censure for abolishing, during the period with which we are now dealing, the feast of Christmas. Strange to say a very important clause in the Ordinance which banned the festivals of Christmas, Easter and Whitsuntide on the grounds of their superstitious usage is forgotten. Yet in connection with the social aspect of the Puritan attitude to Sunday amusements it is a very vital matter. It illustrates for one thing the fact that the people who objected to Sunday sports were not in the main people who would veto all sports upon other days. Yet so often they have been misrepresented as opponents of all amusement. It further shows that the Puritan legislators were willing to provide time for such sport on other days than the Sunday thereby showing, as they did in other points of policy not connected with the present subject, a wisdom in advance of that manifested by many generations of legislators that followed them.

In June 1647 Parliament passed the Ordinance which abolished the festivals already mentioned and also all Holy Days and the Ordinance contained the following clause:[2]

"To the end that there may be a convenient time allotted to scholars, apprentices, and other servants for their recreation: be it ordained by the authority aforesaid That all scholars, apprentices, and other servants shall, with the leave and approbation of their masters respectively first had and obtained, have such convenient reasonable recreation and relaxation from

[1] *Acts and Ordinances*, Vol. I, p. 791.
[2] Ditto, p. 954.

their constant and ordinary labours on every second Tuesday in the month throughout the year, as formerly they used to have on such aforesaid festivals, commonly called Holy Days. And that masters of all scholars, apprentices, and servants, shall grant unto them respectively such time for their recreations on the afore-said second Tuesdays in every month, as they may conveniently spare from their extraordinary and neces-sary services and occasions. And it is further ordained by the said Lords and Commons, That if any difference shall arise between any master and servant concerning the liberty hereby granted, the next Justice of the Peace shall have power to hear and determine the same".

Perhaps to us to-day an indeterminate time on one day a month for relaxation from work does not seem a very praiseworthy grant on the part of Parliament. Anyone who is tempted to belittle what was done should remember that Parliament and public opinion a century ago did not provide for any relaxation at all for any workers in shops or factories and that for such a twelve-hour day for six days a week was the rule. Indeed it was only as recently as 1911 that shop-assistants were able to claim by law any half-holiday in the six-day week. But for the insistence by the Puritan upon no Sunday labour as well as no Sunday sport who knows but what conditions in the early nineteenth century might not have been harder still.

From the point of view of rest from ordinary duties the average citizen under the Puritan regime was definitely better off than he had been or seemed likely to be under the system which the first two Stuart Kings and their clerical advisers had upheld. The Puritan legislators gave him a Sunday free from toil, which he had not been guaranteed before, and took some definite steps to ensure him at least some time for recreation on the week-days.

It may be said that the monthly partial-holiday was only compensation, and perhaps inadequate compen-pensation at that, for the lost freedom of the holy days and festivals. But it must be remembered again that work on such holy days had been permissible after Divine Service was over. We have already noticed the tendency during the seventeenth century towards Sunday labour and that being so one cannot imagine that the tradition of freedom from work upon the holy days would have survived much longer. On the other hand without the definite ban upon Sunday amusements and the abolition of the holy days it difficult to see how any movement towards freedom from toil upon some ordinary working day would have been conceived. The Puritans, therefore, in stopping Sunday work and in providing for some week-day cessation from labour were introducing a very valuable social reform.

There is every indication that Parliament did not find it easy to persuade or compel everyone to observe Sunday according to the new regulations of the Puritan code. For example in March 1649 and again in the September of the same year there were proclamations issued by Parliament and by the Council of State respectively which declared that the existing laws against the profaning of the Sunday must be strictly enforced.[1] In April 1650 Parliament followed up its previous work by yet another "Act for the better Observation of the Lord's Day . . ."[2] This act was particularly directed against Sunday labour showing once more how very difficult it was to secure what on social, quite apart from any religious, grounds was a very essential reform. Shopkeepers crying their goods, butchers, waggoners and drovers are still the chief offenders. All these are once more forbidden to break the peace and rest of the Sunday and all travelling,

[1] *Tudor and Stuart Proclamations*, Nos. 2835 and 2882.
[2] *Acts and Ordinances*, Vol. II, pp. 283-285.

"except it be to or from some place for the service of
God, or upon other extraordinary occasion to be
allowed by the next Justice of the Peace", whether by
water or coach or sedan chair is prohibited. With regard
to other offenders there are still those who drink to
excess upon the Sunday and against these the arm of
the law is once more directed.

We possess some account of the debates upon this
measure in the diary of Thomas Burton who was a member of the Parliament. From his diary it appears that
there were those in Parliament who held the extremely
strict views about Sunday which are the views so often
misrepresented as being those of the whole Puritan
party. For example there appeared in the original
draft of the Bill a clause prohibiting the "idle sitting,
openly, at gates or doors or elsewhere" and the "walking in churchyards".[1] A Mr. West objected to the
clause on the ground that "let a man be in what
posture he will, your penalty finds him". Others
supported his objection, Major-General Whalley observing: "We must take heed to adding to the commandment of God. If you put this clause you deprive men
of the very livelihood they have by the air; as at
Nottingham, many people that have houses in the rock,
and have no air, live most part of their time without
doors". On the other side a Mr. Vincent supported
the clause saying that although it seems "a little
strict" yet "I cannot think such sitting at doors,
as is usual, can be a sanctification of the Lord's day."
The clause was eventually dropped from the Bill by
thirty-seven votes to thirty-five.

A little sidelight such as this is extremely valuable
as it enables us to adjust our view of the attitude of
the Puritans who were in power at this time. Too often
people have remembered the Mr. Vincents among the
Puritans and forgotten the Wests and Whalleys. Although the ultra-strict party could muster a strong

[1] *Diary of Thomas Burton*, edit. Rutt, Vol. II, p. 264.

following the sane and moderate party outnumbered them and, considering the conditions of the times, their enactments read as remarkably sane pronouncements.

In September 1650[1] Parliament repealed the several Statutes of Elizabeth's reign which had enforced attendance at Common Prayer upon the Sunday but the act which did this made it quite clear that all were still expected to attend some place of worship upon the Sunday. In the words of the Act every person, unless he or she had a reasonable excuse, must on the Sunday "diligently resort to some public place where the service and worship of God is exercised, or . . . be present at some other place in the practice of some religious duty, either of prayer, preaching, reading, or expounding the Scripture, or conferring upon the same." This was entirely in keeping with the traditions of the past that attendance at Divine Worship on Sunday was compulsory but it marked a broader view in another direction in the sense that a certain choice of worship was permitted.

Very little was done officially between 1650 and 1657 on the matter of Sunday observance. No doubt this was due to the fact that the essential points had already been covered by existing legislation and what was needed was the enforcement of this legislation rather than the multiplying of it. There is also to be remembered the fact that this was a period of Parliamentary weakness. The last years of the Rump, the days of the Barebones' Parliament and the First Protectorate Parliament were not the times in which to expect much enlightened legislative work. There was a reference to the observance of Sunday in an Ordinance of 28th August 1654 which dealt with the question of ejecting unsatisfactory ministers and schoolmasters.[2] Among the persons described as scandalous are those who are known to be accustomed to "profaning of the Sabbath

[1] *Acts and Ordinances*, Vol. II, pp. 423-425.
[2] Ditto, p. 977.

day, and such as do or shall allow the same in their
families, or countenance the same in their parishioners
or scholars" and it is decreed that "such ministers shall
be accounted negligent as omit the public exercise of
preaching and praying upon the Lord's day (not being
hindered by necessary absence or infirmity of body)".
Instructions were issued to the officials responsible for
the government of the military districts into which
England was at one time divided during the period to
see that, amongst many other laws, those with reference
to Sunday observance were enforced.[1]

In the Humble Petition and Advice of May 1657
among the disqualifications put forward for candidates
for Parliament and members thereof is that of being a
"common profaner of the Lord's day"[2] and in the
following month another Act on the subject of Sunday
observance appeared.[3] This Act must be considered in
some detail because it is the last enactment of the
Commonwealth period which deals exclusively with
the subject of Sunday and it seems to have been
intended to summarize and recapitulate all the previous
legislation on the subject since 1640. The preamble
shows us that there were still those who abused the
sacredness of the day and it is in itself of interest as
setting out the Puritan ground upon which was based
the claim for marking Sunday as a day apart. It says
that a fresh enactment is necessary "forasmuch as God
hath appointed one day in seven to be kept holy unto
himself, and that in order thereupon man should
abstain from the works of his ordinary calling, and
whereas it is found by daily experience that the first
day of the week (being the Lord's day, and since the
resurrection of Christ to be acknowledged the Christian
Sabbath) is frequently neglected and profaned to the
dishonour of Christ."

Then follow clauses very similar to those in previous

[1] *Cal. State Papers Domestic*, Vol. CXXIII No. 19.
[2] *Acts and Ordinances*, Vol. II, p. 1050.
[3] Ditto, pp. 1162-1169.

acts prohibiting waggoners, butchers, bargemen, etc.,
from working on Sunday and forbidding drinking in
taverns or alehouses or the fetching of wines or beer
or tobacco unnecessarily. Following these clauses
comes a much fuller list of trades, etc., which are not
to be engaged in upon the Sunday and this is worth
studying, for presumably it would not have been drawn
up were it not that there were instances of all these
trades being used upon the Sunday in spite of previous
Acts against Sunday work.

This clause reads: "Every person grinding or causing
to be ground any corn or grain in any mills, or causing
any fulling or other mills to work upon the day aforesaid; and every person working in the washing, whiting
or drying of clothes, thread, or yarn, or causing such
work to be done upon the day aforesaid; every person
setting up, burning or branding beet, turf or earth,
upon the day aforesaid; every person gathering of
rates, loans, taxations, or other payments upon the
day aforesaid (except to the use of the poor in the
public collection); every chandler melting or causing
to be melted, tallow or wax belonging to his calling; and
every common brewer and baker, brewing and baking,
or causing bread to be baked, or beer or ale to be
brewed upon the day aforesaid; and every butcher
killing any cattle, and every butcher, costermonger,
poulterer, herb-seller, cordwainer, shoemaker, or other
person selling or exposing or offering to sell any their
wares or commodities, and the person buying such wares
or commodities upon the day aforesaid; all tailors and
other tradesmen, fitting or going to fit, or carry any
wearing apparel or other things; and barbers trimming
upon the day aforesaid; all persons keeping, using, or
being present upon the day aforesaid at any fairs,
markets, wakes, revels, wrestlings, shootings, leaping,
bowling, ringing of bells for pleasure, or upon any other
occasion (save for calling people together for the public
worship), feasts, church-ale, maypoles, gaming, bear-

baiting, or any other sports or pastimes; all persons unnecessarily walking in the church or church-yards, or elsewhere in the time of public worship; and all persons vainly or profanely walking on the day aforesaid, and all persons travelling, carrying burdens, or doing any worldly labour or work of their ordinary calling on the day aforesaid, shall be deemed guilty of profaning the Lord's Day." The penalty for breaking these regulations was a fine of ten shillings for every offender over the age of fourteen and the confiscation of the goods exposed for sale in such cases as infringed the law in that way.

That it was felt necessary to give such a comprehensive list of trades and industries is surely indicative of the widespread extent to which Sunday labour still prevailed and from the social point of view is ample justification for the determination of Parliament to enforce a Sunday rest from daily toil. In few, if any, of the instances cited could there be any excuse for Sunday work. The prohibition with regard to "vainly or profanely walking" is unfortunately vague and open to an over-strict interpretation from the over-zealous Puritan. Apart from this, however, there is nothing in the clauses which, considering the conditions prevailing at the time, was in any way fanatical or an infringement of reasonable liberty.

As in previous Acts provision was made for the reasonable preparation of meals in private houses and inns and for the crying of milk at suitable hours. Thus Parliament gave no sanction to what was after all only the demand of a fanatical minority, that no work of any kind, not even that of preparing a meal, should be countenanced.

The Act prohibited any elections for mayors or aldermen etc., upon the Sunday—another old-time custom which there was every reason for ending. In the same way the serving of writs or warrants except for serious offences such as treason, felony and breach of the peace was to cease. As before the parents, guardians or masters were responsible for the children under fourteen who broke the law. The Act also repeated the injunction that all must "upon every Lord's-day diligently resort to some church or chapel where the true worship and service of God is exercised, or be present at some other convenient meeting-place of Christians, not differing in matters of faith from the public profession of the nation as it is expressed in the Humble Petition and Advice of the Parliament to His Highness the Lord Protector." Finally it enacted "that all persons contriving, printing or publishing any papers, books, or pamphlets for allowance of sports and pastimes upon the Lord's day, and against the morality thereof shall forfeit the sum of £5."

That Parliament was particularly determined to end Sunday labour is seen not only by the Act but by a clause in an Act which was issued at the same time and which dealt with the improvement of the collection of excise and other duties. The clause in question reads: [1]

"That if any common brewer of beer or ale, soap-boiler, or distiller of aqua-vitae or strong-waters, shall at any time upon the Sabbath day brew or tonne any beer or ale, boil or make any soap, or distil or make any aqua-vitae or strong waters" he shall forfeit double the value of what he has made.

This ended the legislation of the Commonwealth period on the subject of Sunday observance. If one reviews all that Parliament had done between 1640 and 1660, particularly if one has come to the matter with the impression that the Puritans when in power were "kill-joys" and the imposers of grievous burdens upon the people, one is amazed at the saneness and moderation of the legislation dealing with the Sunday question. It was simply the logical development of the trend of the thought of the more enlightened legislators and administrators of the previous half-century. It was

[1] *Acts and Ordinances*, Vol. II, p. 1194.

neither revolutionary nor reactionary. Far from being harsh and narrow it was socially beneficial and progressive. The Puritans are often charged with being extremely individualistic. The story of their legislative efforts on the matter of Sunday observance is an exception to this indictment, if it be an indictment. For the Puritans showed themselves to be keenly alive to the social danger of allowing people to please themselves as to whether they worked upon the Sunday or not, just as they were aware of the social evil that resulted from the liberty, which so often had degenerated into licence, to amuse oneself for part of the Sunday very much as one pleased, regardless of the inconvenience, not to say danger, to which others were thereby exposed.

Whatever may be said about the views or the conduct of individual Puritans on the matter of Sunday observance—and the extremists then as now often achieved the greatest publicity—it is certain that their legislative efforts on the matter are deserving of praise and not censure. That they built soundly and in keeping with the tendency of the past was vindicated by the fact that so little of what they did was lost when they fell from power and their opponents triumphed.

CHAPTER XI

THEORY AND PRACTICE—1640 TO 1660

HAVING studied the attitude of Parliament towards
Sunday observance during the period of Puritan power,
we must now attempt to discover what the feelings
and actions of the ordinary people were like during the
same space of time. After the stifling of opinion on all
matters during the latter part of the Eleven Years'
Tyranny people welcomed the opportunity of greater
freedom of criticism which came in 1640. On matters
of religion this criticism was frequently voiced before
the special Committee of Religion which was set up by
the Long Parliament in 1640. This committee received
frequent complaints of the harm which had been
done by the re-issue by Charles I of his father's Declaration of Sports, as well as evidence to show that those
who had refused to read the Declaration had suffered
persecution. The chairman of this committee was Sir
Edward Dering, and he has left on record many of the
letters and petitions connected with the business of
the committee which he received. Several of these
have point for the subject we are considering.

In a letter to Dering from a certain William Barret
dated November 2nd, 1640, the latter refers to "the
profanation of the Lord's Day" as one of the four great
national sins.[1] A petition against episcopacy forwarded
to Dering by Mr. Richard Robson on behalf of the
people of Kent refers to "the faintheartedness of
ministers to preach the truths of God, lest they should
displease the prelates" and amongst "the truths" he

[1] *Proceedings . . . in . . . Kent*, p. 21.

classes "the Sabbath".[1] The same petition puts to the debit account of the bishops "the profanation of the Lord's Day, pleading for it, and enjoining ministers to read a declaration set forth (as it is thought by their procurement) for the toleration of sports upon that day, suspending and depriving many godly ministers for not reading the same, only out of conscience that it was against the law of God so to do, and no law of the Land enjoining it".[2] This petition is an example of the way in which the bishops, by their attitude to the matter of Sunday games, had given those in the State who disliked episcopacy an additional weapon with which to attack them.

The parishioners of Tonbridge sent a petition against their vicar and included in the charges against him is the statement that he "is a man of a profane life and conversation, being so far from restraining others from using sports on the Lord's Days, that he himself will stand at his door and see young people at their sports, and laugh at them".[3] Evidently the freedom to indulge in Sunday amusements was not welcomed by all the people, and one imagines that the influence for good of such a man as the Vicar of Tonbridge must have been negligible.

There was still a great lack in the country of clergy who would take their duties seriously. Many of the people were appealing for more religious instruction, but too often their appeal fell on deaf ears. The parishioners of Maidstone, then a town of some six thousand people yet possessing only one Parish Church, complain against Robert Barrell who was the curate-in-charge for the Archbishop of Canterbury, who was the vicar. The curate only preached once a month or so, and when absent provided unsatisfactory substitutes. The people "have offered to choose an able man, and to maintain him at our own charge, who might take pains to instruct

[1] *Proceedings . . . in . . . Kent*, p. 30.
[2] Ditto, p. 35.
[3] Ditto, p. 193.

us in the afternoons on Sabbath days (necessary occasions hindering servants and others in the forenoon) yet he refuseth; by reason whereof much ignorance, lewdness, and disobedience doth reign among us. . . . He is not only negligent himself to preach, but hath also rebuked a painful neighbouring minister for preaching twice on the Sabbath days, telling him that (he) did much disgrace the clergy by preaching twice on the Sabbath days; and that preaching in the afternoon was but prating and babbling".[1] This is an illustration of how far short some, at any rate, of the clergy were falling, by 1640, of the ideal visualized by the early reformers and legislators of the Church. Small wonder if the people in such a parish abused the liberty of the Sunday and necessitated the passing of restrictive legislation.

It must not be supposed, of course, that all the clergy were as neglectful of their duties as Robert Barrell. No doubt many followed the ideal expressed a few years before by George Herbert, when he wrote of the parson on Sunday going to church with his family after private devotions at home and "having read Divine Service twice fully, and preached in the morning, and catechized in the afternoon, he thinks he hath in some measure, according to poor and frail men, discharged the public duties of the congregation. The rest of the day he spends either in reconciling neighbours that are at variance, or in visiting the sick, or in exhortations to some of his flock by themselves, whom his sermons cannot or do not reach".[2] If all had followed this plan, it might not have entirely prevented the need for the Sunday legislation of the Puritan regime, but it would have made its scope simpler and its enforcement easier. On the other hand, such men as Herbert describes had prepared the minds of many for the acceptance of such legislation as was found neces-

[1] *Proceedings . . . in . . . Kent*, p. 203.
[2] G. Herbert: *A Priest to the Temple*, p. 25.

sary, just as the neglect of the Barrells had helped to
create the situation which Parliament tried to remedy.

If, during the period which followed the second issue
of the Declaration of Sports, the clergy had in some
instances allowed undue laxity upon the Sunday, the
magistrates also in certain cases were equally culpable.
For example, certain gentlemen petitioned Parliament
in 1640 against Thomas Lane, the Recorder of the
borough of Wycombe and a Justice of the Peace because
he "advanced the profanation of the Sabbath by sports
and games he countenanced". [1]

Thus in 1640 there was clearly both the need for a
stricter oversight in connection with the observance of
Sunday and the desire on the part of many that this
oversight should be enforced by Parliament. That
Parliament was not slow to interpret the wishes of the
country on the matter we have seen in the previous
chapter.

In 1641 appeared a very moderately-worded defence
of the Puritan position on the matter of Sunday observance by Dr. William Twisse. In this book he very aptly
says what might be more carefully considered to-day by
those who still hold a biassed view of the Puritan
attitude to Sunday, namely: "We show no more zeal in
saying that the Lord's Day is by some licentiously profaned than others do in professing that the Lord's Day
is by us superstitiously observed." [2] Twisse discredits
many of the stories prevalent in books attacking the
Puritan position which depict the ultra-rigid observance
of Sunday. On the matter of amusements he says: "To
deal plainly, my opinion is, that all sports and pastimes
on the Lord's Day are a breaking of the rest belonging
to it, and a profanation of that day which ought to be
sanctified; and I trust herein I differ not one jot from
the whole parliament Ist Caroli". That statement sums
up the Puritan position on the matter in 1640 very

[1] D'Ewes: *Journal of the Long Parliament*, p. 513.
[2] Wm. Twisse: *Of the Morality of the Fourth Commandment*, p. 188.

clearly. It was not some new and revolutionary doctrine which they initiated. They merely desired a logical continuance of the progress of the past, a progress which had been arrested and retarded for some dozen years.

Towards the end of 1644 the Assembly of Divines at Westminster were discussing the preparation of a directory for the observation of the Sabbath. Some account of its deliberations on the subject appears in the works of one of its members, Dr. John Lightfoot. Amongst other propositions on the subject it was agreed "to abstain from all unnecessary labours, worldly sports, and recreations" on the Sunday, and it was decided after some debate to add "worldly thoughts".[1] Some opposition being aroused to the suggestion that no feasting be allowed on Sunday, it was agreed "that the diet on the Sabbath-day be so ordered that no servants or others be unnecessarily kept from the public service".[2] It was agreed that people be encouraged to prepare themselves privately for Divine Worship before setting out for church, and to aim at a timely arrival there. Finally it was agreed that "what time is vacant in the whole day from the public worship should be spent in reading, singing, repetitions, etc."[3] There is nothing in all this which suggests any great departure from the King's Book of 1543, or the Homily of the Place and Time of Prayer issued in 1574. If a minority of over-zealous Puritans chose to read more drastic restrictions into the legislation of Parliament, or the directions of the Assembly of Divines, that should not allow, as it too often has, the real position of the Puritans to be obscured or misread.

Naturally, during the period of the Civil War, for those engaged in the armies in the field any careful observance of the Sunday as a day of rest and worship was impossible. Apart from necessary movements of troops and the routine duties of camp life, skirmishes

[1] *Works of John Lightfoot*, edit. Pitman, Vol. XIII, p. 328.
[2] Ditto.
[3] Ditto, p. 329.

and battles could not be avoided just because it happened to be the Sunday. Richard Baxter tells us of hearing the cannon sounding at the battle of Edgehill while preaching on the Sunday afternoon.[1] Many instances of the movements of troops and military activities on the Sunday are given in Richard Symonds' *Diary of the Marches of the Royal Army during the Great Civil War.* On a May Sunday in 1647, Major-General Skippon was busy holding a conference with some of the officers of the Parliamentary forces about certain grievances of the army, the conference actually taking place within the Parish Church at Walden.[2] Considering the views which we have seen Charles I held on the question of Sunday observance, it is not surprising that he and his army did not restrict themselves to entirely necessary movements on the Sunday. Thus on Sunday, June 2nd, 1644, we read: " At one of the clock in the afternoon the king, accompanied with his troop etc. went to Woodstock and killed two bucks, and supt there ",[3] the royal headquarters being at the time at Oxford.

The whole of the country was not the scene of constant warfare or of military occupation all through the Civil War, and in such places as remained for long or short intervals outside the sphere of military operations, the general observance of the Sunday was, on the whole, improving. Daniel Neal, in his *History of the Puritans*, gives a very glowing account of the state of affairs when he writes: " It is certain that the laws against vice and immorality were strictly executed, the Lord's Day was duly observed, the churches were crowded with attentive hearers, family devotion was in repute, neither servants nor children being allowed to walk in the fields, or frequent the public-houses. In a word, notwithstanding the difference of men's opinions and political views, there was a zeal for God and a much

[1] Baxter: *Autobiography*, p. 41.
[2] *Clarke Papers*, Vol. I, p. 45.
[3] Symonds: *Diary*, p. 7.

greater appearance of sobriety, virtue, and true religion than before the Civil War, or after the blessed Restoration".[1]

Neal is writing here of conditions about 1647. No doubt where there were conscientious ministers who shepherded and instructed their people and where there were faithful magistrates to see that the law was enforced, such a description as Neal gives correctly describes the state of affairs. But it would be a mistake to trust too confidently Neal's conclusion. Had all been as he describes, the later legislation and the later enforcements of the law would not have been necessary. There were still many places where the Sunday was not by any means as carefully observed—places where the royalist influence was predominant and places where careless or inefficient guardians of the public morals allowed the wilder elements in society full vent for their impulses. Thus we get such conditions as prevailed in 1646 at Crediton in Devon, where an order was made at the Midsummer Sessions to enforce a stricter observance of the Sunday because "the Lord's day . . . is profaned by many lewd people, and not kept and observed in many places as it ought to be".[2] In the same year an order was made by the Judges at the Dorchester Assizes, following a complaint made by the Grand Jury, to suppress many of the alehouses because of the disorders they occasioned "especially on the Sabbath days, whereby the service of Almighty God is much hindered".[3]

The Diary of the Rev. Ralph Josselin, Vicar of Earles Colne in Essex, shows us how the fortunes of war might upset the orderly Sunday routine of a place. Under the date June 11th, 1648, he writes: "The enemy marched on to Braintree die: 10: and this day, being up and down, plundering and taking away Mr.

[1] Neal: *History of the Puritans*, Vol. III, p. 403.
[2] Hamilton: *Quarter Sessions*, p. 138.
[3] *History of Liquor Licensing* by S. and B. Webb, p. 12.

Nicholson two miles beyond us upward to Colchester; our people assembled in arms; we were not able to draw into Church for the keeping the Sabbath, but were deprived of that opportunity".[1] The entry for Sunday, July 2nd, 1648, reads: "I preached at home, and so I did every Lord's Day that month, and on the first day: we were not troubled with one alarm, but the carts went continually to the leagues, and so did persons, that there was no distinction made of Sabbath, so that war truly is ready to make people more vile, a rare thing to see men made better".[2] Josselin seems to have been a fairly typical seventeenth century parson, sincere and hard-working, a supporter of Parliament, but one who did not favour extreme measures such as the execution of the King. No doubt his experience was that of countless other ministers during the Civil War, and there would surely be few to-day who would question the accuracy of the conclusion he arrived at as to the influence of warfare on man's character. Probably too little regard is given by many of the critics of the Puritan regime during the Commonwealth to the degenerating effect of the previous years of warfare upon a great number of the people.

The relaxation of even the age-long customary methods of observing the Sunday as a day of worship, brought about by the abnormal conditions of war-time coming so soon after the period when people had been encouraged to a great degree of freedom once the religious services were ended, must have meant that the Sunday was very slightly regarded by many people by the middle of the seventeenth century. This in its turn would seem to justify those who had a genuine regard for the value and sacredness of the day, who sought to hedge in all that they esteemed best in the day by stringent regulations. That many had ceased to pay much regard to the obligations of the Sunday is illus-

[1] *Diary of Josselin*, p. 50.
[2] Ditto, p. 52.

trated by a well-known passage from John Bunyan's
Grace Abounding. Although well-known it is so pertinent to the present inquiry that it will bear repeating.
Bunyan, writing of events in his life about 1649 or
1650, at a time when he was a regular attendant twice
a Sunday at Divine Worship says: "One day, amongst
all the sermons our parson made, his subject was, to
treat of the Sabbath-day, and of the evil of breaking
that, either with labour, sports or otherwise. Now I
was, notwithstanding my religion, one that took much
delight in all manner of vice, and especially that was a
day that I did solace myself therewith". The sermon
impressed Bunyan, but the impression faded with the
enjoyment of his dinner and he "shook the sermon out
of my mind, and to my old custom of sports and gaming
I returned with great delight". He had not finished with
the sermon though, for "the same day, as I was in the
midst of a game at cat, and having struck it one blow
from the hole, just as I was about to strike it the second
time, a voice did suddenly dart from heaven into my
soul, which said: 'Wilt thou leave thy sins and go to
heaven, or have thy sins and go to hell?'"[1] Bunyan
ceased his play to wrestle with the idea, but eventually
returned to his play, believing himself too great a
sinner to be forgiven.

From this incident it is clear that, in some villages at
any rate, the people were still free to indulge themselves
much as they pleased after Divine Service was over.
Also the account shows how necessary it was, if any
reform of Sunday observance was to be secured, that
Parliament should legislate strictly on the matter and
that its laws should be enforced. The mere preaching of
the doctrine of a Sunday free from work and sport was
insufficient. Even though the people were compelled to
listen to such teaching it might prove ineffective. Bunyan was led to consider his ways, but even this consideration did not lead him immediately to mend his

[1] Bunyan's *Grace Abounding*, § 20, 21 and 22.

ways: there must have been many who heard but who refused even to consider.

There is plenty of evidence to show that, even during the period of the Commonwealth, there was need for a stricter enforcement of law and order on the Sunday than often prevailed. Those who imagine that under the Puritan rule every town and village was a peaceful, orderly, albeit dull, place, have in their minds a picture which is not by any means always based upon reality. A few examples, drawn from different parts of the country, showing the conditions that prevailed, will prove this.

The Quarter Sessions for the North Riding of Yorkshire at the meeting at Kirkby Moorside on July 10th, 1649, ordered: "Upon a petition preferred by the ministers of Thornton in Pickering Lythe, Kirkby moorside, Edston, Lastingham, and Helmesley, and other ministers in the North Riding, of the great profanation of the Lord's Day in and through the said Riding, and the ordinance of parliament, for the suppressing of vice and punishing of offenders, neglected by the constables and churchwardens, who are to see the same put in execution, to the great dishonour of God and discouragement of painful and laborious ministers, the constables are required from time to time to take special care the said Ordinance of Parliament for better observance of the Lord's Day, and penal statutes in that case provided, be put in due execution, by carrying the offenders before the next justice of the peace to receive condign punishment". [1]

The Quarter Sessions for Wiltshire in 1647 had to suppress certain alehouses at Barford St. Martin and Stanton Bernard because they tended to the "profanation of the Sabbath". [2]   In 1652 the Session Records show that "Information is laid against various persons of Woodborough, Cannings, and Marlborough, who

---

[1] *Quarter Session Records*, edit. J. C. Atkinson, Vol. V, p. 33.
[2] *Hist. MSS. Commission*: Report for 1901, p. 113.

assembled with muskets, bandaleers, swords etc. on the Lord's Day, May 16, and finally, with a drummer and fiddler, numbering in all about 300, went in a riotous and warlike manner to Pewsey, and there very disorderly danced the Morris dance, drinking and tippling till many of them were drunk".[1]

In 1650 the Justices of the Peace at Taunton had to deal with complaints from the parish of Merriott against an inn-keeper "of the great disorders and abuses committed on the Lord's Day and other days".[2] In this case the offender was forbidden to sell ale or beer to any but travellers. Two years later a petition was sent to the Quarter Sessions by the minister of Chesilborough, which states: "Whereas there is an act made by this present Parliament for the better keeping and observing the Lord's Day, and whereas the Lord's Day is greatly profaned at West Chinnock within this parish aforesaid, usually every Lord's Day, by sports and pastimes prohibited, in regard that the officers of that place who are concerned in the said act do not only neglect, but altogether refuse to do their duty in that behalf, whereby God is highly dishonoured and the young people in licentiousness encouraged. The premises considered your petitioner doth humbly desire that some course may be taken with the officers aforesaid according to the said act".[3]

In 1654 a certain Samuel Hayland was disqualified from sitting as a burgess for Southwark, and among the charges made against him was one that, in his capacity of a justice of the peace, he had condoned the fines of profaners of the Sunday.[4] About the same time charges were made against a certain Hum. Orme that, when he was a magistrate, he discouraged complaints of profaning the Lord's Day.[5]

---

[1] Hist. MSS. Commission: Report for 1901, p. 126.
[2] Somerset Quarter Session Records, edit. Harbin, Vol. III, p. 127.
[3] Ditto, p. xlvii.
[4] Cal. State Papers Dom. 1654, Vol. LXXIV, No. 69.
[5] Ditto, No. 88.

As the country settled down more after the unrest
of the Civil War, it became more easy to enforce the
legislation dealing with the observance of Sunday and
this, coupled with the increasing influence of the
ministers, led to a more satisfactory condition of affairs.
Even so, there were always those who would evade or
break the law if they could. The cases that came before
the magistrates, however, were, generally speaking, of
such a nature that the offenders deserved restraint or
punishment because their offences were of an anti-
social order and not merely a defiance of unpopular
religious restraint. Thus we find the Yorkshire magistrates fining a man fifteen shillings at Richmond in
1652 "for playing at bowls, and other unlawful games,
and selling tobacco upon the Lord's Day".[1] Two years
later they have before them "a Reeth yeoman for
selling oatmeal, peas and tobacco on the Lord's Day".[2]
Three months later at Thirske they deal with "a
Thorneton Beanes woman for suffering people to drink
and play in her house in the Sabbath day . . . a
Newbrough woman for being a common drunkard and
profaner of the Sabbath".[3] The records of Canterbury
for 1654-55 contain a reference to the fining of a certain
John Johncock for selling shoes on the Sunday.[4] The
records of Plymouth show the following presentments
made by the constables on January 9th, 1659. "Jno.
Olde for keeping men drinking yesterday, being Lord's
day. Jno. Wood, servant to Mr. Anthony Skinner for
walking on the Hoe sermon-time. Several vagrants
who came yesterday to town sermon-time to beg.
George Cragg for suffering company in his house to
drink burnt wine sermon time".[5] In the latter case it
should be noted that the offences of Wood and Cragg
would have been punishable a century previously in

---

[1] *Quarter Session Records*, edit. Atkinson, Vol. V, p. 113.
[2] Ditto, p. 163.
[3] Ditto, p. 168.
[4] *Hist. MSS. Commission*, Ninth Report, p. 165.
[5] Ditto, p. 266.

so far that their absence at "sermon-time" presumably implies their non-attendance at any part of Divine Worship.

It has already been shown in this book that Sunday work and Sunday sport were in almost all cases calculated to injure the right of the citizen to a restful and quiet Sunday, and offences under those categories may therefore fairly be classed as anti-social. Perhaps some may not agree that travelling upon the Sunday fell into that class also. Here, however, we would remind the reader that when considering the legislation on the subject we have pointed out how unnecessary Sunday travelling was in the majority of cases, and that the liberty to travel, when enjoyed, was frequently abused by the carriers and others in such a way as to cause an offence to peaceful citizens and that even when this was not so, Sunday travelling in most cases caused unnecessary labour. No doubt there were cases, perhaps many cases, where fanatical informers and narrow-minded magistrates caused unnecessary inconvenience and injury to genuine travellers. Yet in many other cases travellers who had any claim to consideration were fairly treated. For example, the Mayor of Coventry in 1655 records in his diary for December 9th: "The lady Archer send her men from Warwick to buy linkes to bury her son, who died last night of the pox and could not be kept longer than this night. Being the Lord's Day, I was in doubt whether Wheler, her man, might not be punished for breach of the Sabbath, but consulting Mr. Piddock, Mr. Bassnet and Dr. Grew, they resolved I might let him pass".[1] On the following 6th of January he writes: "Being Lord's Day John Haw brought one Brisco who lives at Corley, to me for coming on foot hence; he alleged that he came to church here and that there was no sermon at Corley. Whereupon I took security from Ger. (?) Cooke, baker,

---

[1] Quoted in article in *Transactions of Royal Hist. Soc.* Fourth Series, Vol. III, p. 113.

that if Brisco proved there was no sermon at Corley then he should be free, otherwise to pay 10d.".[1]

On the other hand the Mayor put three Quakers in the cage for travelling on Sunday, presumably without good reason although, as he stated "it grieved me that this poor deluded people should undergo punishment of such a nature".[2] Josselin, mentioned previously, the vicar of an Essex village, records in his diary for October 17th, 1658: "Our officers punish some travellers, a new work with us"[3] so that either there were not would-be travellers to be found all over the country or it was a long time before the officials in some parts of the country took any action against them. In 1655 John Manley, the Postmaster-General, complained to the Council that on the previous Sunday the post who carried the mail from London to Barnet had the horse he was riding seized by the constable of Highgate. In this case the Council gave orders for the restoration of the horse to its owner.[4] Here was a case where even though the local officials had interpreted the law narrowly it was possible to obtain redress by applying to higher authority showing that it was no intention of the responsible legislators and administrators that the Sunday regulations should be unduly irksome.

In Thomas Ellwood's story of his own life an incident is given which may serve to illustrate the fact that the regulations about travelling were not always enforced so tyrannically as is often represented. Ellwood was a Quaker, a member of an unpopular sect at that time, and one Sunday early in 1660 he set out to journey from Reading to Chalfont. At Maidenhead he was stopped by the watch and taken before the chief offices of the town. Asked why he travelled on Sunday Ellwood reports that he replied: "I did not know that it would give any offence barely to ride or walk on that day, so

[1] Quoted in article in *Transactions of Royal Hist. Soc.* Fourth Series, Vol. III, p. 113.
[2] Ditto.
[3] Josselin's *Diary*, p. 126.
[4] *Cal. State Papers Dom.* 1655, Vol. XCIV, No. 32.

long as I did not carry or drive any carriage or horses laden with burdens." He was told that if his business were urgent he should have obtained a pass from the mayor of Reading. Then, as it was Church-time, the Warden sent Ellwood under the charge of the constable to the Greyhound Inn to await further examination. Ellwood explained that he had no money—even the horse he was riding and the riding-coat he was wearing had been borrowed—but orders were given to the people to be civil to him. After dinner his examination was continued and he was finally told that although he had incurred the penalty of a fine or several hours in the stocks he would be discharged and he was escorted out of the town by a second constable. Ellwood's own comment is: "Through the town I rode without further molestation; though it was as much Sabbath, I thought, when I went out as it was when I came in." [1]

No doubt Ellwood would have fared worse in many towns. Yet such an incident seems to show that possibly the rigidness of the Puritan administration has been over-stressed and that where we do get records of the penalties being harshly enforced the cases were such as admitted of no reasonable excuse for the breach of the law. Ellwood himself could not have complained or even have expected sympathy had he received the punishment which the law allowed, for he had obviously not complied with the law, possibly through a misapprehension of its meaning as he suggests, by obtaining a pass for his journey.

The ten years or so which followed the close of the Civil War gave the faithful ministers of the Word a greater opportunity than they had had before to instruct and influence their people in religious matters. The teaching with regard to the separation of the Sunday from all unnecessary work and from all sport which had gone on in many parts of the country for many years before the Civil War, and which had been

[1] *Life of Thomas Ellwood*, edit. Crump, pp. 42-48

rudely broken into upon occasion in many places during the Civil War, was then more widespread. This, coupled with the legislation of the Long Parliament and other Assemblies, meant that the work of individuals, of groups of people impressed with the necessity of a quiet Sunday on social and religious grounds, of magistrates, of Parliament itself reached its consummation.

No doubt the picture which Richard Baxter gives of Kidderminster just before and after the Civil War would be increasingly true of many other parts of the country by the close of the Commonwealth period. Baxter says: " On the Lord's Days there was no disorder to be seen in the streets, but you might hear an hundred families singing psalms and repeating sermons as you passed through the streets. In a word, when I came thither first (in 1641) there was about one family in a street that worshipped God and called on his name and when I came away (1660) there were some streets where there was not passed one family in the side of a street that did not so, and that did not, by professing serious godliness, give us hopes of their sincerity. And those families which were the worst, being inns and alehouses, usually some persons in each house did seem to be religious ". [1]

After this description of Baxter's it may be worth while to give a little attention to the views which Baxter himself held of the correct observance of Sunday. He set them out in a lengthy treatise called *The Divine Appointment of the Lord's Day Proved*. He believed that the Sunday ought to be spent chiefly in public worship and that any time left over from this should be spent in family devotions. He has several very pertinent things to say on the matter of Sunday work and Sunday sport—things which are worth studying when trying to estimate the ideas of the thoughtful man of the period on the subject. He puts the Puritan

[1] *Autobiography of R. Baxter*, p. 79.

view very clearly and fairly when he says: "I pray you deal openly, and tell me, you that think a day too long for God, and are weary of all holy work, what would you be doing that while, if you had your choice? Is it anything which you dare say is better? Dare you say that playing is better than praying, or a pipes or dancing better than praising God with psalms? Or that your sleep, or games, or chat, or worldly business is better than the contemplation of God and glory! And will those deceivers of the people also say this, who teach them that it is a tedious, uncommanded thing to serve God so long? I think they dare not speak it out. If they dare, let them not grudge that they must for ever be shut out of heaven, where there will be nothing else but holiness. But if you dare not say so, why will you be weary of well doing, that you may do ill? Why are you not more weary of everything than of holiness, unless you think everything better than holiness". [1] Men may falter at the challenge and cry out that ordinary mortals cannot attain to the heights to which rare spirits would aspire, but let them at least admire the lofty vision and not decry it as narrow or joyless.

Remembering the social conditions of the time, Baxter has some shrewd words to say on the matter of Sunday sport. He knows that a specious plea is often made for Sunday recreation for those who are labouring hard for six days of the week and he answers it thus: "But the truth is, it is not the minds of poor labouring men that are overworked and tired on the week-days, but it is their bodies: and therefore there is no recreation so suitable to them as the ease of the body, and the holy and joyful exercise of the mind upon their Creator, their Redeemer, and their everlasting rest". [2] Then follows a significant suggestion. If sports and recreations are necessary, says Baxter, "let the land-

[1] *Practical Works of Baxter*, edit. Orme, Vol. XIII, p. 437.
[2] Ditto, p. 445.

lords abate their tenants as much rest, as one day's vacancy from labour in a month or a fortnight will amount to, or let the common Saints' days, which of the two are more at man's disposal, be made their sporting-days, and rob not their souls of that one weekly-day, which God had separated for his worship".[1] There comes the practical suggestion which, from the social point of view, was to improve the conditions of the worker far more than any attempt to secure for him Sunday games. As for students and lawyers and gentlemen who need recreation, "there are few of these so poor but they can take their bodily recreation on the week-days".[2] Baxter knows well that rules may be too rigid and he would have discretion used in determining the matter of Sunday recreation. Thus he says: "No bodily recreations are lawful which needlessly waste time, or hinder our duty, or divert our minds from holy things, or are a snare to others. Unless it be some weak person whose health requireth bodily motion, few persons need any other than holy recreation on that day. . . . But I will not censure one whom I see walking at fit hours, when for ought I know he may be taken up in some fruitful meditation. But if persons will walk in the streets or fields in idleness, or for vain delight, or discourse, as if the day were too long for them, and they had no business to do for their souls, this is not only a sin, but a very ill sign of one that is senseless of his soul's necessity and his duty".[3]

With reference to the matter of Sunday labour Baxter is no less clear. He gets socially to the heart of the problem when he says: "The tyranny of many masters maketh the Lord's Day a great mercy to the world: for if God had not made a law for their rest and liberty, abundance of worldly impious persons would have allowed them little rest for their bodies, and less

[1] *Practical Works of Baxter*, edit. Orme, Vol. XIII, p. 446.
[2] Ditto.
[3] Ditto, p. 457.

opportunity for the good of their souls".[1] Baxter shows us something of the conditions of life for many people at that time when he pleads that if the ordinary people do not get religious instruction upon the Sunday, they will never get it. His statement is: "The poverty, servitude, and worldly necessity of the most, do require a strict observation of the whole Lord's Day. Tenants and labourers, carters and carriers, and abundance of tradesmen are so poor, that they can hardly spare any proportion of time: much less all their children and servants, whose subjection, with their parents' and masters' poverty, restraineth them. Alas! they are fain to rise early and hasten to their work and scarce have leisure to eat and sleep as nature requireth: and they are so toiled and wearied with hard labour, that if they have at night a quarter of an hour to read a chapter and pray, they can scarce hold open their eyes from sleeping. What time hath the minister then to come and teach them? (if we had such ministers as would be at the pains to do it) And what time have they to hear or learn? You must teach them on the Lord's Day or scarcely at all. Almost all that they must learn must be then learned".[2]

As with recreation so with work, Baxter would have people use their discretion. He would not ban the necessary duties of the day such as the preparation of meals, urgent travel he would allow, the saving of cattle or crops from flood is permitted. Here an apt illustration puts his case very clearly. Baxter says: "If I see a man that unexpectedly findeth some uncomely hole or rent in his clothes, either pin it up or sew it up, before he goeth abroad, I will not blame him: but if he do it so as to embolden another who useth needlessly to mend his clothes on the Lord's Day, it will be a sin of scandal".[3]

There can be no doubt that for Baxter, and many like

[1] *Practical Works of Baxter*, Vol. XIII, p. 462.
[2] Ditto, p. 461.
[3] Ditto, p. 456.

him, the Sunday was a truly joyful day. To accuse such
men of wishing to make it a day of gloom and penance
is to be woefully ignorant of their aims and actions.
That all might not find in the duties of the day such a
joy as Baxter found is understandable. At the same
time it must be remembered that men of Baxter's way
of thinking had found little or no joy in the noisy
Sundays that so many had had to endure in certain
parts of the country in the period prior to the Civil War.
Probably the licence of the Sunday devoted in part to
sport or labour was responsible for conditions which
aroused the disapproval of at least as large a section of
the community as the one which felt itself aggrieved
under the regime of the Puritans while there was at any
rate this to be said for the latter, that they were
adopting an attitude, whether they realized it or not,
calculated to improve the social conditions of all the
people. Baxter's views upon the Sunday show too,
as did the legislation of the period as we have seen, that
there was nothing fanatical or extreme about the
position taken up by the responsible Puritan.

Objection has sometimes been made that the Puritan
ban upon Sunday games led to the rise of a working
class which knew not how to play games. It has
already been shown that the Puritan legislation carefully made provision for the setting aside of certain
time upon the week-day for sport. Baxter himself,
although not one who looked with much favour upon
sport at any time, made the suggestion that masters
should give their employees time for recreation upon
the week-day. The same idea is expressed in some
verses written probably about the beginning of the
Civil War by Robert Heywood, a Lancashire man.
He wrote:

" Playing upon the Sabbath days
    To breed distractions in the mind

Yea, full as much and many ways
As work or worldly thoughts, I find:
Then rest thy mind (instead of play)
In God, and sport another day."[1]

That is to say, the man who opposed Sunday games
was not necessarily opposed to all games. If less time
was given to sport in the future it was not the fault of
the Puritan so much as the employer, of whatever
religious school, who refused to give permission for
time to be given to sport upon the week-day.

Probably, too, the loss is over-estimated. We have
repeatedly seen that the leisure time upon the Sunday,
even when the Declaration of Sports was in force, was
too frequently devoted either to creating a noisy disturbance or to sitting drinking in the alehouse. Many
of the so-called sports were not such as would confer
any physical or moral benefit upon either participator
or spectator. On the other hand, such sports as were
healthy and enjoyable were not stamped out, as the
following account given in the autobiography of the
Honourable Roger North shows. North is writing of
the year 1658 and the conditions then prevailing in
Kirtling, which place he describes as consisting of
"tillage farms and small dairies, so that business was
usually done by noon, and it was always the custom
for the youth of the town, who were men or maid
servants, and children, to assemble, after horses baited,
either upon the green or (after haysel) in a close accustomed to be so used, and there all to play till milking
time and supper at night. The men to football and the
maids, with whom we children commonly mixed, being
not proof for the turbulence of the other party, to stool-
ball, and such running games as they knew".[2] That is
to say, where time allowed upon the week-day there was
no attempt to prevent indulgence in games.

---

[1] *Observations and Instructions Divine and Morall* by R. Heywood, Century 3rd,
verse 63.
[2] *Autobiography of Roger North*, p. 9.

CHAPTER XII

THE PERIOD OF THE RESTORATION

§1. THE ATTITUDE OF THE CAVALIER PARLIAMENT TO THE SUNDAY QUESTION

THOSE who have assumed that the idea of a Sunday divorced from work and sport originated in this country with the Puritans of the Commonwealth period have always been puzzled to explain how it was that the keeping of Sunday in that way did not cease in 1660. If such people were to give any consideration, as usually they do not, to the views of the Cavalier Parliament on the subject they would be still more hard pressed to explain the situation. The Cavalier Parliament was most decidedly anti-Puritan if by Puritan is meant one who dissents from the doctrines of the Anglican Church. In many cases it was anti-Puritan if by the term Puritan is meant one who advocates a stricter line of moral conduct than the normal. Yet in spite of this not only did this Cavalier Parliament do nothing to re-establish the freedom to sport as one wished upon the Sunday but it took steps to see that in the main the position achieved by the legislation of the Commonwealth period with regard to a quiet and restful Sunday was maintained.

On the other hand those who have followed the steady development of thought on the matter of Sunday observance which has been going on ever since the time of the Reformation and which it has been one of the purposes of this book to trace out will not be surprised at the attitude of the Cavalier Parliament. Going

back as it did to the Acts of 1625 and 1627 it was able
in its own work to embody the experience gained by a
knowledge of the work done in the Commonwealth
period without it seeming that it was acting in any
Puritanical fashion. Indeed nothing can be clearer than
the fact that the Cavalier Parliament regarded the idea
of a Sunday free from toil and noisy amusement as one
of the old Parliamentary traditions and not as a whim
of recent growth. Thus, although the enactments of
the period from 1641-1660 ceased to operate, steps were
taken to see that the Sunday continued to be observed
quietly.

Before coming to the work of the Cavalier Parliament
it will be necessary to see that the Convention Parliament which preceded it, and which was the Parliament
to welcome Charles II back, took steps to consider this
question of Sunday observance. As early as July 20th,
1660 the House of Commons "Resolved that the King's
Majesty be humbly moved, that he will please, by
his Proclamation, to quicken the execution of all laws
in force against the breaking of the Lord's Day,
Drunkenness, Swearing and other profaneses." [1] Apparently the King did not act on the suggestion and
that is probably why on August 11th the House of
Commons read for the first time a Bill dealing with
Sunday observance. On September 12th the House
of Commons again desired the King "to declare his
dislike of the profanation of the Lord's Day; and also
to command the Justices of the Peace, and all other
public ministers of justice in their several places to do
their duties for preventing and suppressing the like
profanations for the future". [2] Nothing came of this
and the Commons proceeded with their Bill which was
sent to the House of Lords in November. It received a
second reading in the House of Lords and was sent to
Committee [3] but it got no further before Parliament was

[1] *Journals of House of Commons*, Vol. VIII, p. 95.
[2] Ditto, p. 168.
[3] *Journals of House of Lords*, Vol. XI, p. 211.

dissolved at the end of the year. Difficulty in any case
seems to have arisen during the committee stage
judging from a letter written by a certain Edwards
referring to the House of Lords sticking at the Bill.[1]
Yet it is significant that the measure got so far. Evidently opportunity was being taken by some people to
throw off the restraint which had been imposed during
the Commonwealth and equally evident is the fact that
the House of Commons was anxious that something at
any rate of the quietude and rest which people had
grown accustomed to on the Sunday should be preserved.

We can now turn to the attitude and work of the
Cavalier Parliament which met in 1661. On April 30th,
1662 the House of Commons "Ordered, That Sir Robert
Holt, Sir Francis Goodrick, Mr. York, and Mr. Pryn,
do peruse the old laws touching the observation of the
Lord's Day; and bring in a new Bill to supply any
defects therein; and to provide for the better observing
thereof; and that no arrests be made on that day, but
penalties imposed on such as shall presume to do it."[2]
This Bill received a second reading in May but was then
apparently laid aside and in any case Parliament was
prorogued until the following February. On May 19th
the House of Commons also asked the King to issue a
proclamation for the proper observance of the Sunday
but again the King did not act. In March 1663 the
Bill, or a fresh one, reached the Committee stage in the
House of Commons but then was laid aside as
apparently the Committee could not agree over certain
amendments.[3] The next month five members were
instructed to prepare a new Bill. The House of Commons, if it had difficulty over details, was evidently
agreed upon the main issue, namely that a measure to
improve the observance of Sunday was essential, otherwise it would not have devoted so much time to the

[1] *Cal. State Papers Dom.* 1660, Vol. XXIV, No. 43.
[2] *Journals of House of Commons*, Vol. VIII, p. 417.
[3] Ditto, p. 456.

subject. This new Bill apparently met with approval
for it had passed through all its stages by the beginning
of June.[1] It quickly received the approval of the House
of Lords also except for certain amendments which they
made which cannot have been drastic, because the
House of Commons accepted them all and returned
the Bill to the Lords.[2] That this Bill never became
law seems to have been due to a very singular incident.
The Clerk of the House of Lords after the return of the
Bill to that House from the House of Commons informed the House "That the bill for the better observation of the Lord's Day hath been, during the sitting
of the House, taken from the table, and is not now to
be found."[3] The Clerk explained that several members
of the House had been at the table and had taken a
number of Bills out of the bag containing them and had
scattered them all over the table. When they were
eventually collected up the Bill dealing with Sunday
observance could not be found. Each member then
present in the House was called upon to declare whether
or not he knew anything of the matter and all denied
any knowledge. As however this inquiry was not made
until the afternoon session when several peers, who had
been present in the morning when the incident had
occurred, were not present, the result was inconclusive.
Apparently no further steps were taken in the matter
and the Bill was never recovered and the reason for its
disappearance remains a mystery. Thus what had
seemed to be an agreed measure never reached the
Statute Book in 1663.

For the next six or seven years the House of Commons
was continually considering Bills on the matter of
Sunday observance but they were all dropped before
they had completed their course in the Lower House.
Thus Bills obtained a second reading and were sent to

[1] *Journals of House of Commons*, Vol. VIII, p. 496.
[2] Ditto, p. 515.
[3] *Journals of House of Lords*, XI, p. 577.

Committee in March 1664,[1] January 1665[2] and October
1667[3] while the question of bringing in a suitable Bill
was considered in October 1666 but nothing then came
of it.[4] So evidently the House of Commons was alive
to the necessity of further Sunday regulations but was
unable to decide upon the exact form which such regulations ought to take. By April 1671 agreement seems to
have been reached and a Bill which had been introduced
the previous year was passed and sent to the House of
Lords.[5] It reached the Committee stage in the House
of Lords on April 20th[6] but the prorogation of Parliament two days later for a period of twelve months put
an end to the life of that Bill. In March 1673 another
Bill was introduced in the House of Commons but only
obtained a first reading and was then dropped.[7] In
October 1675 the House of Commons set up a committee
to bring in another Bill "for the better observation of
the Lord's Day"[8] but no report of the committee is
recorded. The Journals of the House of Commons fail
to supply any evidence as to the reasons which led to
so many of these attempts to improve the observance
of Sunday being abortive. It is clear however that
many in both Houses must have been anxious to improve the general conduct of the people on the Sunday
or all these attempts would not have been made or have
succeeded to the extent to which they did.

While during all this period Parliament had been
unable to agree upon legislation there had been one
proclamation dealing with the matter. On August
22nd, 1663 a royal proclamation enforced the observance
of the laws compelling people to attend church and
forbade assemblies for unlawful pastimes, and the

[1] *House of Commons' Journals*, Vol. VIII, p. 539.
[2] Ditto, p. 581.
[3] Ditto, Vol. IX, p. 9.
[4] Ditto, Vol. VIII, p. 636.
[5] Ditto, Vol. IX, p. 234.
[6] Lords' Journals, XII, p. 507.
[7] Commons' Journals, IX, p. 270.
[8] Ditto, p. 360.

travelling of carts or waggons; drinking; and the selling of goods on the Sunday.[1]

In March 1677 the House of Lords took up the matter and brought in a Bill "for the better observation of the Lord's Day, called Sunday."[2] This Bill was received by the House of Commons from the House of Lords on April 13th and three days later it had passed through all its stages in the Lower House[3] and it received the royal assent the same day. The chief points in this Act are as follows:[4]

"That all the Laws enacted and in force concerning the observation of the Lord's Day, and repairing to the Church thereon be carefully put in execution; and that all and every person or persons whatsoever shall on every Lord's Day apply themselves to the observation of the same by exercising themselves thereon in the duties of piety and true religion, publicly and privately; and that no tradesman, artificer, workman, labourer, and other person whatsoever shall do or exercise any worldly labour, business or work of their ordinary callings upon the Lord's day, or any part thereof (works of necessity only excepted); and that every person being of the age of fourteen years or upwards, offending in the premises shall for every such offence forfeit the sum of five shillings; and that no person or persons whatsoever shall publicly cry, shew forth, or expose to sale any wares, merchandises, fruit, herbs, goods or chattels whatsoever upon the Lord's Day, or any part thereof, upon pain that every person so offending shall forfeit the same goods so cried or shewed forth or exposed to sale.

"And it is further enacted that no drover, horse-courser, waggoner, butcher, higler, they or any of their servants, shall travel or come into his or their inn or

---

[1] *Cal. State Papers Domestic* 1663, Vol. LXXIX, No. 28. Tudor and Stuart Proclamations, p. 408.
[2] *Lords' Journals*, XIII, 56.
[3] *Commons' Journals*, IX, pp. 421 and 423.
[4] *Statutes at Large*, Vol. V, p. 436.

lodging upon the Lord's Day or any part thereof, upon pain that each and every such offender shall forfeit twenty shillings for every such offence; and that no person or persons shall use, employ or travel upon the Lord's day with any boat, wherry, lighter or barge, except it be upon extraordinary occasion, to be allowed by some Justice of the Peace of the County. . . .

"Provided that nothing in this act contained shall extend to the prohibition of dressing of meat in families, or dressing or selling of meat in inns, cooks' shops, or victualling houses, for such as otherwise cannot be provided, nor to the crying and selling of milk before nine of the clock in the morning and after four of the clock in the afternoon."

Amongst other points the Act also enacted that hundreds could not be held responsible for travellers who were robbed on the Sunday and that warrants and writs must not be served on that day except in a case of treason, felony or break of the Peace.

If this Act be compared with those of 1625 and 1627 it will be seen that such changes or advances as are made are those which the experience of the Commonwealth period had shown to be desirable and necessary. For example the Act of 1677 makes it quite clear that no person at all is to pursue his ordinary occupation upon any part of the Sunday. This is a much more definite statement than any in the two previous Acts. On the other hand the matter of Sunday amusements and sport is not dealt with, it apparently being clear that all that is necessary is contained in the previous Acts and that there is no need to reiterate the prohibitions therein contained. The influence of the years of Puritan rule had, to a great extent, done its work in that direction and there was not the need for fresh legislation. That is to say the main feature of the Act of 1677 was to enforce the social benefit of rest from ordinary toil, the social advantage of a more peaceful

Sunday in the matter of disturbing amusements having
already been achieved. Thus the Act of 1677 was the
natural sequence to the Acts of 1625 and 1627 and was
in this sense parallel with the numerous measures of the
years 1642 to 1660. So did a Parliament which certainly could not be termed Puritan in any sense of that
word confirm and complete the work which Parliament
had been striving to do ever since the days of Elizabeth.
Sunday was definitely pronounced to be a day set apart
from the other days of the week: a day upon which
ordinary work must not be performed: a day which
must not be spoilt by noisy amusements: a day the
whole of which should be devoted to private and public
worship and deeds of charity. This was translating, as
far as legislation could do it, into actual practice what
the early Reformation documents had set out as the
ideal theory. Long experience had shown that the
theory would not be turned into practice by many
people of their own free will. It had also shown that
socially a Sunday partly given over to sport or work
was a danger. Hence apart from any narrow Puritanical
creed the legislation of 1677 saw the necessity for and
the value of enforcing a quiet, restful Sunday.

§2. THE ORDINARY OBSERVANCE OF SUNDAY IN THE REIGN OF CHARLES II

JUST as we have seen Parliament after 1660 anxious to
preserve almost in its entirety the method of observing
Sunday which had become habitual with many during
the Commonwealth, so we shall find the local authorities
equally zealous in the same cause. For example the
records of the County of Hertford show us several

cases of prosecutions for working upon the Sunday or
for profaning it in some other way. Thus in 1661 a
shoemaker at Hemel Hempstead, who was also the
constable, was summoned for selling shoes on Sunday.[1]
The following year a butcher at Buntingford was presented for killing and dressing meat on Sunday.[2] In
1663 a cordwainer of Hitchin appeared on the charge of
selling shoes on Sunday.[3] A carpenter of Barley was
presented "for profaning the Sabbath day in being
drunk and not coming to Church 29 April 1666."[4] In
this last case it will be noticed that the word "Sabbath"
is still used—a word which as we have seen had been
introduced by those who desired a stricter observance
of the Sunday than that officially enforced in Elizabeth's reign and one which had come to have definite
association with the Puritans. In 1670 a coachman of
Cheshunt was presented for "entertaining of several
sorts of persons in sermon time to the profaning of the
Sabbath day."[5] In 1675 a silk weaver of Cheshunt was
summoned because on the Sunday he opened his shop and
sold goods.[6] The attempt on the part of some to resume
work upon the Sunday seems to have been particularly
persistent for John Gates of Throcking, a butcher, was
summoned in 1676 and again in 1678 for selling meat
on Sunday.[7] The Act of 1677 did not immediately put
an end to these attempts at Sunday labour for we find
records of presentments for working upon the Sunday
after that date as for example the summoning of
higglers for travelling on Sunday in 1682[8] and the
summoning of a butcher for Sunday trading and a
labourer for Sunday work in the fields in 1683 and 1692
respectively.[9]

[1] *Hertford County Records*, Vol. I, p. 139.
[2] Ditto, p. 145.
[3] Ditto, p. 156.
[4] Ditto, p. 183.
[5] Ditto, p. 222.
[6] Ditto, p. 253.
[7] Ditto, pp. 270 and 278.
[8] Ditto, p. 316.
[9] Ditto, pp. 330 and 401.

There are examples to show that similar conditions prevailed in other parts of the country. Josselin, whose diary of events in the Essex village of Earles Colne has already been referred to, has the following entry for March 1st, 1663: "Some in our town were digging this Sabbath morning, Lord whither will this profaneness tend? To flat atheism. Lord arise, help for thy mercy sake."[1] It was this sort of thing which caused the magistrates and Parliament to act as they did. Where they did not act promptly, and one judges that the district where Josselin lived was such an area, the people tended to relapse into slacker ways. Thus Josselin's entry for June 12th, 1664 is: "This day, a day of holy rest, is now the sport and pleasure day of the general rout of people."[2] In 1663 the Corporation of Trinity House took steps to prevent Sunday labour, for an order dated the 27th of July ordered that "notices be fixed in the most public places forbidding persons licensed by the Corporation to row in wherries to work on the Sabbath".[3] The Quarter Sessions held at Richmond, Yorkshire, on January 18th, 1670 had to deal with "Nine Burtyeside yeomen for playing football on the Lord's day in the time of divine service; five Hardrawe yeomen for the like . . . two Aperside yeomen for buying and selling wool on the Lord's day; a Bainbridge man for selling soap and tobacco on the Lord's day; a Sedbuske man for selling suits of apparel on the Lord's day."[4] Thomas Ellwood in his autobiography records the punishment in London in 1662 of a man imprisoned for breaking the law by Sunday labour. He writes: "He was a very poor man, who lived by mending shoes and on a seventh-day night, late, a carman, or some other such labouring man, brought him a pair of shoes to mend, desiring him to mend them that night, that he might have them in the morning,

[1] Josselin's *Diary*, p. 143.
[2] Ditto, p. 145.
[3] *Historical MSS. Commission*, Eighth Report, p. 251.
[4] *Quarter Session Records*, edit. Atkinson, Vol. VI, p. 141.

for he had no other to wear. The poor man sat up at
work upon them till after midnight, and then finding he
could not finish them, went to bed, intending to do the
rest in the morning. Accordingly he got up betimes and
though he wrought as privately as he could in his
chamber, that he might avoid giving offence to any,
yet could he not do it so privately but that an ill-
natured neighbour perceived it, who went and informed
against him for working on the Sunday."[1]

One good result of all the previous years of struggle
for a more distinctive observance of Sunday was certainly the fact that the majority of people were more
accustomed to regard Sunday labour as wrong. Those
who concede this benefit sometimes claim that it is
more than outweighed by the loss in facilities for and
therefore knowledge of and skill in sport. This point
has been touched on at the end of the last chapter. Here
it will be sufficient to add that there is nothing to show
that the average Englishman in the reign of Charles II
was any the less ardent in his pursuit of sport, or any
the less adept in its various branches, than his ancestors.
Indeed the evidence is the other way. Edward Chamberlayne writing of the state of England in the reign
of Charles II says: "For variety of divertisements,
sports and recreations no nation doth excel the
English."[2] After referring to the hunting, hawking,
horse-racing, bowls, tennis and many other recreations
of the nobility Chamberlayne says: "The citizens and
peasants have hard-ball, football, skittles or nine-pins,
shovel-board, stow-ball, goffe, trol-madam, cudgels,
bear-baiting, bull-baiting, bow and arrow, throwing
at cocks, shuttle-cock, bowling, quoits, leaping, wrestling, pitching the bar and ringing of bells, a recreation
used in no other country of the world."[3] There is no
sign of any diminution in sport.

Every writer on social conditions in the reign of

[1] *Life of Ellwood*, p. 102.
[2] *Angliæ Notitia* by E. Chamberlayne, p. 52.
[3] Ditto, p. 53.

Charles II must perforce be under a great sense of indebtedness to Samuel Pepys. Any attempt in the present connection to give an exhaustive list of the references in Pepys' Diary to the way in which Pepys and those he knew spent their Sundays would be tedious to the reader and would tend to obscure rather than throw light upon the present study. But some space must be found for a certain number of quotations and for certain broad conclusions which are the result of an examination of all the references to Sunday which Pepys records. In giving these quotations the date of the entry will be set down and this, rather than any reference to the particular page of any edition of the diary, will provide the easiest method of verification. January 1st, 1660 was the first Sunday for which an entry is given and this records what in many ways was a typical Sunday for Pepys, in so far as any day in the life of a man with such varied interests could be called typical. On that day Pepys attended Divine Worship in the morning, looked at his accounts in the afternoon, and visited his father in the evening. The habit of devoting some part of the Sunday to his own private accounts was one which is frequently noted in the diary and from it Pepys slipped fairly easily later into that of devoting part or all of the day to public business also. Pepys was a frequent worshipper but judging by his practice of visiting various city and other churches it was by no means imperative, notwithstanding the law, to attend one's own Parish Church upon the Sunday, at any rate for citizens of London. In the same way Pepys seems to have found little difficulty in travelling frequently in London and its environs upon the Sunday. No doubt the size of London made it impossible, in many cases at any rate, to observe as strictly as in other places those people who absented themselves from their Parish Church or who travelled further afield upon the Sunday than necessity demanded.

For February 5th, 1660 Pepys has the entry: "In

the Court of Wards I saw the three Lords Commissioners sitting upon some action." Either the uncertain state of the country or extreme pressure of business was presumably the cause of a departure from the correct observation of the Sunday on that occasion. Over against this may be set an entry for the following Sunday which says: "Walking with Mr. Kirton's apprentice during evening church, and looking for a tavern to drink at, but not finding any open, we durst not knock." Pepys and the apprentice were themselves breaking the law but it is significant that in accordance with the law all the taverns were closed. This too, be it noted, at a time when the general state of London was one of excitement due to the activities of General Monk and the uncertainty as to what form of government was to be brought into operation.

The entry for Sunday, April 7th, 1661 reads: "All the morning at home making up my accounts (God forgive me!) to give up to my Lord[1] this afternoon. Then put in at Paul's where I saw our minister, Mr. Mills, preaching before my Lord Mayor. To White Hall, and there I met with Dr. Fuller of Twickenham, newly come from Ireland; and took him to my Lord's, where he and I dined; and he did give my Lord and me a good account of the condition of Ireland. . . . After dinner, my Lord and I and Mr. Shepley did look over our accounts, and settle matters of money between us; and my Lord did tell me much of his mind about getting money, and other things of his family." The pious ejaculation in the record seems to show that Pepys could not entirely divorce himself from the atmosphere which the period of the Commonwealth had taught people to associate with Sunday. Therein lay a great deal of the value of the work of the Puritans. Everyone, now that conditions were not so strict, would not refrain from Sunday work—but even among those

---

[1] "My Lord" here and elsewhere in the Diary means Admiral Sir Edward Montagu, later Earl of Sandwich.

who did work many would feel uncomfortable in so doing and would realize that what they did was not a normal thing. On the other hand there would be those who would welcome the passing of the strict enforcement of some of the Sunday restrictions and here again Pepys gives us an interesting entry with reference to a Mr. Creed who had once been a zealous Puritan. On Sunday, May 12th, 1661 after attending service at the Savoy Pepys writes: "Met with Mr. Creed, with whom I went and walked in Gray's Inn walks, and from thence to Islington, and there ate and drank at the house my father and we were wont of old to go to; and after that walked homeward, and parted in Smith-field: and so I home, much wondering to see how things are altered with Mr. Creed, who, twelve months ago, might have been got to hang himself almost as soon as go to a drinking-house on a Sunday."

The habit of conducting private devotions in the home on the Sunday which the Puritans had cultivated was one which prevailed even with a man of Pepys's stamp after the Restoration, for on Sunday September 29th, 1661 Pepys indulged over-much in wine at dinner and supper and consequently was forced to record "so home and to bed, without prayers, which I never did yet, since I came to the house, of a Sunday night."

Pepys seems to have been something of a "sermon taster"—or perhaps it was his delight in seeing a pretty face which he mentions more than once as if it were his primary object in attending service—for of March 16th, 1662 he writes: "This morning, till churches were done, I spent going from one church to another, and hearing a bit here and a bit there." It must be remembered that the hours of Divine Worship were still at this time very much earlier than those customary to-day. For example on August 17th, 1662 Pepys talks of arriving at St. Dunstans at 7 a.m. and finding the church not open he walked in the Temple-gardens until 8 a.m. when the church was half full. In the afternoon he was only able to find standing room in the gallery at one o'clock. The crowd on that occasion was due to the fact that Dr. Bates, a well-known minister, was preaching his farewell sermons before being deprived of his pulpit under the terms of the Act of Uniformity. On the 9th of November Pepys was again making a round of the churches and he records that he was "observing that in the streets and churches the Sunday is kept in appearance as well as I have known it at any time." This latter statement is very significant coming from such a shrewd observer as it testifies to the fact that there had been no violent reaction from the way in which the Sunday was kept under the Puritan regime. That it was the intention of the authorities in Church as well as in State to see that there was no serious departure from the method of keeping Sunday which had grown customary is shown by another reference Pepys gives in connection with the previous September 14th. He writes: "By water to White Hall, by the way hearing that the Bishop of London had given a very strict order against boats going on Sundays, and as I come back again we were examined by the masters of the company, in another boat, but I told them who I was." The last part of the statement is no doubt the clue which explains why Pepys himself so often seemed to be able to do what the ordinary citizen was forbidden to do upon the Sunday.

Those who had any connection with the royal Court or any office under a State department were almost bound to find themselves called upon to depart from the idea of a quiet, restful Sunday, at least upon some occasions. Charles II, like his father, was evidently one who saw no reason why, the public devotions for the day having received a perfunctory attention, the Sunday should not be spent as any other day. His residence on the Continent would have increased what would be his natural tendency of thought following his early environment. He had had no experience of the change of attitude towards the Sunday which his subjects had grown into and to which they had become accustomed. The atmosphere of the Court therefore on the Sunday was a very different one from that of the rest of the nation. It is a commentary upon the different attitude adopted by Charles II towards his people's wishes from that adopted by Charles I that Charles II did not attempt to force his conception of the way Sunday should or might be kept upon his people at large. There was no new declaration of sports although no doubt Charles II would have had every sympathy with such a document.

Abundant evidence is furnished by Pepys of the way in which Charles II and his ministers transacted State business upon the Sunday. Thus on Whitsunday in 1662 after attending Divine Worship twice the entry records: "Thence to the Council chamber; where the King and Council sat till almost eleven o'clock at night, and I forced to walk up and down the galleries till that time of night. They were reading all the Bills over that are to pass to-morrow at the House, before the King's going out of town and proroguing the House." On January 28th, 1666, a Sunday, the entry is: "Took coach, and to Hampton Court, where we find the King, and Duke, and Lords, all in council." On Sunday, October 7th, 1666 we read: "To White Hall . . . to attend the King and Duke of York at the Cabinet." A fortnight later the entry is: "To White Hall, and there attended the Cabinet, and was called in before the King, and then to give an account of our want of money for Tangier." On Sunday, January 24th, 1669 Pepys was roused from sleep with an order to attend on the King in the afternoon. Pepys attended morning service and then after dinner went to Whitehall. From there he had to accompany the Court to Essex House near the Temple. "Here all the Officers

of the Navy attended, and by and by were called in
to the King and Cabinet . . . and the business was to
know in what time all the King's ships might be
repaired, fit for service." Many similar entries to
those just given will be found by those who are
interested in searching the diary.

Apart from attendance at Court Pepys seems to have
found that pressure of official business required him to
work at his office on the Sunday fairly frequently.
Reference has already been made to this and among
additional instances are these. On October 23rd, 1664:
"To church. . . . At night to the office, doing business,
and then home to supper. Then a psalm, to prayers,
and to bed." On November 27th after attending
church in the morning Pepys is at the office in the
afternoon. The entry for November 24th, 1667 is: "For
want of other of my clerks, sent to Mr. Gibbs, whom I
never used till now, for the writing over of my little
pocket Contract-book; and there I laboured till nine
at night with him . . ." Sunday, March 28th, 1669
was filled with business at the office all the day until
eight in the evening. These entries could be supple-
mented by many of a similar nature.

The tendency to spend part or all of the Sunday in
private or public business was one which increased as
the years, recorded in the diary, passed and corres-
pondingly, as almost invariably is the case, a growing
inclination to devote part of the day to pleasure may be
noted. Thus on Sunday, April 14th, 1667 Pepys writes:
"Took out my wife, and the two Mercers, and two of our
maids, Barker and Jane, and over the water to the
Jamaica House, where I never was before, and there
the girls did run for wagers over the bowling-green;
and there, with much pleasure, spent little, and so
home." On the 14th of July in the same year Pepys
and his wife and a Mrs. Turner went by coach to
Epsom for the day, leaving soon after 5 a.m. and getting
home about 11 p.m. True Pepys attended Divine

Worship on their arrival at Epsom but the remainder of the day was spent in resting at the inn, talking with friends, and walking in the woods and on the Downs. On the evening of the following Sunday—there is no record for the morning and afternoon—Pepys and his wife went "up by water to Barne Elmes, where we walked by moonshine, and called at Lambeth, and drank and had cold meat in the boat, and did eat and sang, and down home, by almost twelve at night, very fine and pleasant, only could not sing ordinary songs with the freedom that otherwise I would." On August 11th a visit was paid by coach to Barnet and Hatfield, the church service at the latter place being attended. After a good dinner the party walked in the park and then returned by coach to Barnet where they remained a while and then proceeded home by coach. Seeing how much time work and pleasure was occupying on the Sunday in 1667 we are not surprised to read for April 5th, 1668: "To Church, where I had not been a good while."

There are suggestions in the diary that others, besides those forced by their official position to work upon the Sunday, failed to keep the day as one of rest from ordinary work. On Sunday, January 14th, 1666 Pepys lay "long in bed, till raised by my new tailor, Mr. Penny, who comes and brings me my new velvet coat." On Sunday, November 4th is "my tailor's man brings my vest home, and coat to wear with it, and belt and silver-hilted sword." After visiting Whitehall on Sunday, February 18th, 1666 Pepys "took coach, and home, calling by the way at my book-seller's for a book." On the other hand there were those who would not consider secular things upon the Sunday as is instanced by the entry for January 27th, 1667 which reads: "To Sir Philip Warwick, by appointment, to meet Lord Bellassis, and up to his chamber, but find him unwilling to discourse of business on Sundays: so did not enlarge."

One could continue to glean from the diary many similar references to illustrate Pepys habits upon the Sunday. Pepys was not a typical Londoner of his age and therefore his habits must not be taken as typical of the general customs of the time. Yet a study of such entries as have been set down here throws considerable light upon the conditions under which Sunday was observed in the early years of the reign of Charles II. An individual in a privileged position could evidently spend the day much as he pleased, yet there were few such persons in comparison with the whole population and it is quite clear that there was a general absence of much of the noisy behaviour and irreverence which had so often marked the Sunday in, say, the reign of James I or of Charles I.

Similar evidence to that given by Pepys with regard to the conduct of State business on Sunday can be found in the Diary of John Evelyn. For example on Sunday, July 9th, 1665: "I went to Hampton Court, where now the whole Court was, to solicit for money; to carry intercepted letters; confer again with Sir Wm. Coventrie, the Duke's Secretary; and so home, having din'd with Mr. Secretary Morice." The entry for September 17th of the same year is: "Receiving a letter from Lord Sandwich of a defeat given to the Dutch, I was forced to travel all Sunday."

§3. CONCLUSION

THE survey which we have now completed shows that by the end of the reign of Charles II certain broad principles with regard to the observance of Sunday had emerged. First of all the State, in the interests of social well-being rather than at the dictate of any par-

ticular school of religious opinion, had seen fit to ban
unnecessary Sunday labour. In so doing it was acting
in harmony with traditions which had existed and
developed since the early days of the Reformation.
The ideal of the early Protestant reformers that men
should discipline themselves upon the Sunday had
proved itself impossible of attainment. The State had
seen that a *laissez-faire* attitude towards the keeping
of Sunday was open to far too many abuses. Some
measure of control was a social necessity and that
measure of control, in the light of various experiments
and previous enactments, it sought to impose in the Act
of 1677.

Secondly public opinion had been educated into a
new conception of the value of Sunday observance.
Not only Sunday labour but Sunday sport was felt by
the majority of the people to be out of place. They had
been led to this conclusion by a lengthy process of
experiment. The Declarations of Sports and the most
restrictive of the Puritan Ordinances had been the
opposing limits of the experiments and from it all
people had emerged with the feeling that restriction was
preferable to license. But on this point Public opinion
did not need to the same extent as in the case of
Sunday labour the backing of the Law, for the period
of the Commonwealth had left a strong religious tradition, that prevailed even amongst those who were not
Nonconformists, that the Sunday was a day to be spent
more quietly than was compatible with any indulgence
in the rough or noisy or brutal sports of the period.

Perhaps this idea of Sunday as a *quiet* day was the
predominant note in the harmonious conclusions which
had been arrived at concerning the proper way in which
to spend the day. The noisy butcher, player, tippler
and traveller had all incurred censure so often that the
majority of people were at last able to attain to something like peace upon the Sunday. If the Court or the
individual, in the privacy of his own home, had to tran-

sact business at any rate it would be done quietly and the general public would be almost, if not entirely, unaware of it and undisturbed by it. Regarded from the religious point of view it might, to some minds, be unsatisfactory that there should be exceptions to the general rule of a Sunday free from work. But socially, provided those who worked did not disturb those who had no desire to work and did not compel, as a general rule, those to work who needed and wished for a quiet day, the position was a big advance upon previous conditions. Perhaps on this point we are in the gravest danger to-day of under-estimating the value of the Sunday as observed by the time of the reign of Charles II and, because we do not realize this value, of sacrificing the rest and quiet of the old type of Sunday which is needed more than ever in the feverish rush of the present time.

The idea of Sunday as a day free from work and noisy pleasure was, as we have seen, based on various grounds. In so far as it was a religious idea it was built upon a misconception of the force of the Fourth Commandment in a Christian community. But men had been driven to take up that position in order to find some authority upon which to found their claims for a new observance of the day. The State Church had been unwilling to use its authority for that purpose, so some other had been required. That they did seek to interpret the Jewish law of the Sabbath to fit the conditions of their own day was only a parallel action with that which at the same time interpreted Magna Carta to suit the political needs of the time. We do not despise to-day the liberties which were won by the supporters of Parliament in the seventeenth century because some of those liberties were based upon a mis-reading of the feudal charter of 1215. We should, therefore, not fail to admit the value of the work of those who used the Fourth Commandment as a Charter of Liberty from Sunday labour and as a pledge of a peaceful day.

But apart from the religious grounds there were moral and social grounds which warranted the enforcement of a restful Sunday and the social reformer should not deny his approval to those who struggled for such an aim in their desire to better the lot of the ordinary people. As so often religious reformer and social reformer were helping to bring about the same end although they were probably not conscious of that fact and might have refuted the suggestion that they were in any sense co-workers.

The danger of rules and restrictions is that they become either fetters through inelasticity or a theme of ridicule through non-observance. To what extent the rules fencing in the observance of Sunday which existed either in State command or Church custom or Public Opinion at the end of the reign of Charles II were destined to succumb to either alternative it is outside the scope of this book to consider. But whatever might be the subsequent story of Sunday observance in England there is no doubt that those who created and developed the tradition which prevailed by 1677 are deserving of the gratitude of posterity on moral, social and religious grounds.

The English Sunday after over a century of experiment was the work of no narrow-visioned section of society but of the best in all sections and schools of thought that had the well-being of their country in view. Sunday had been made a distinctive day of rest. The value of that from the social, quite apart from the religious, point of view cannot be over-estimated.

BIBLIOGRAPHY

THE following books have been consulted in the preparation of this study and quotations from or direct reference to the majority of them will be found in the text.

A. Books and documents written during the sixteenth and seventeenth centuries including modern editions of such works.

ASSHETON—The Journal of Nicholas Assheton of Downham for 1617-1618, edited F. R. Raines (Chetham Society).

BARWICK, JOHN—A Summary Account of the Holy Life and Happy Death of Thomas Late Lord Bishop of Duresne, edition of 1660.

BAXTER, RICHARD—The Autobiography of Richard Baxter, edited J. M. Lloyd Thomas.

—The Divine Appointment of the Lord's Day Proved: Vol. XIII of The Practical Works of the Rev. Richard Baxter, edited Wm. Orme, Vol. XIII, edition of MDCCCXXX.

BACON, NATHANIEL—The Official Papers of Sir Nathaniel Bacon of Stiffkey, Norfolk as Justice of the Peace 1580-1620, edited H. W. Saunders (Camden Society).

BEAKE, ROBERT—Extracts from the MS. Diary of Robert Beake, Mayor of Coventry 1655, from article by Miss M. D. Harris in Transactions of the Royal Historical Society 1920.

BECON, THOMAS—Writings of the Rev. Thomas Becon.

BRAMSTON, JOHN—The Autobiography of Sir John Branston, K.B., of Skreens 1611-1700 (Camden Society).

BUNYAN, JOHN—Grace Abounding, edited E. Venables, edition MDCCCC.

BURTON, THOMAS—Diary of Thomas Burton, Esq., M.P., 1656-1659, edited J. T. Rutt, Vol. II.

CALENDAR OF STATE PAPERS—Domestic Series—Volumes covering period.

CANONS—The Constitutions and Canons Ecclesiastical of the Church of England, edited M. E. C. Walcott.

CHAMBERLAYNE, EDWARD—Angliœ Notitia or the present State of England, edition of 1676.

CHAMBERLAIN, JOHN—Letters written by John Chamberlain during the reign of Queen Elizabeth, edited S. Williams (Camden Society).

CLARKE, WILLIAM—Selections from the papers of Wm. Clarke, Secretary to the Council of the Army 1647-49, Vol. I, edited C. H. Firth (Camden Society).

COMMONS—Journals of the House of Commons—Volumes covering the period.

—Debates in the House of Commons in 1625; edited S. R. Gardiner (Camden Society).

CRANMER, THOMAS—Remains, of Thomas Cranmer, edited H. Jenkyns, Vol. IV, edition of MDCCCXXXIII.

DERING, EDWARD—Papers and Letters sent to Sir Edward Dering contained in Proceedings principally in the County of Kent . . . in 1640 and especially with The Committee of Religion, edited L. B. Larking (Camden Society).

D'EWES, SIMONDS—A Complete Journal of the Votes, Speeches and Debates both in the House of Lords and House of Commons throughout the whole reign of Queen Elizabeth, edition of MDCXCIII.

—Journal of Sir Simonds D'Ewes from the beginning of the Long Parliament to the opening of the trial of the Earl of Strafford, edited Wallace Notestein.

DYSON, HUMPHREY—A Book Containing all such Proclamations as were published during the reign of the late Queen Elizabeth, edition of 1618.

ELLWOOD, THOMAS—History of the Life of Thomas Ellwood . . . by his own hand, edited C. G. Crump.

EVELYN, JOHN—Diary, edited W. Bray.

FOX, GEORGE—The Journal of George Fox, edition of 1901.

FRITH, JOHN—Declaration of Baptism contained in The Works of Wm. Tyndale and John Frith, edited T. Russell, Vol. III.

FULLER, THOMAS—The Holy State and The Profane State, edited J. Nichols.

—The Appeal of Injured Innocence, edition MDCLIX.

—The Church History of Britain, 3rd edition, edited J. Nichols, Vol. III.

GOSSON, STEPHEN—The School of Abuse (1579), edited E. Arber.

GREENHAM, RICHARD—A Treatise of the Sabbath—edition of 1612.

GREY FRIARS—Chronicle of the Grey Friars of London, edited J. G. Nichols (Camden Society).

HARLEY, BRILLIANA—Letters of the Lady Brilliana Harley, edited T. T. Lewis (Camden Society).

HAYWARD, JOHN—Annals of the First Four Years of the Reign of Queen Elizabeth (Camden Society).

HERBERT, GEORGE—A Priest to the Temple, edition of 1671.

HEYLYN, PETER—The History of the Sabbath, edition of 1636.

HEYWOOD, ROBERT—Observations and Instructions Divine and Morall in verse, edited T. Crossley (Chetham Society).

HISTORICAL MANUSCRIPTS—Reports of the Historical Manuscripts Commission: particularly the 3rd, 4th, 5th, 8th, 9th and 15th reports: the Calendar of the MSS. of the Dean and Chapter of Wells: the MSS. of Lord Kenyon: the MSS. in various collections in the 1st volume for 1901.

HOMILY OF THE PLACE AND TIME OF PRAYER—Contained in Formularies of Faith put forth by Authority during the reign of Henry VIII, edition of MXCCCXXV.

HOOKER, RICHARD—Works, edited I. Walton, arranged J. Keble, Vol. II, edition MXCCCXLI.

HOOPER, JOHN—Early Writings of John Hooper, edited S. Carr.

HUSBAND, EDWARD—A Collection of all the Public Orders, Ordinances and Declarations of both Houses of Parliament 1642-1646, edition of 1646.

JOSSELIN, RALPH—The Diary of the Rev. Ralph Josselin 1616-1683, edited E. Hockliffe (Camden Society).

KING'S BOOK—"The King's Book" of 1543 or A Necessary Doctrine and Erudition for Any Christian Man, contained in Formularies of Faith (see reference above under Homily).

LANCASHIRE—The Lancashire Lieutenancy under the Tudors and Stuarts, edited John Harland (Chetham Society).

LANCASTER—A Description of the State, Civil and Ecclesiastical of the County of Lancaster about the year 1590 by some of the Clergy of the Diocese of Chester, contained in the Chetham Miscellanies, Vol. V (Chetham Society).

LIGHTFOOT, JOHN—Works, edited J. R. Pitman, Vol. III, Vol. XIII of edition of MDCCCXXI.

LODGE, THOMAS—A Defence of Poetry, Music and Stage-Plays, edition of 1853.

LORDS—Journals of the House of Lords, volumes covering period.
—Notes of the Debates in the House of Lords, officially taken by Henry Elsing 1624 and 1626, edited S. R. Gardiner (Camden Society).

MACHYN, HENRY—Diary of Henry Machyn 1550-1563, edited J. G. Nichols (Camden Society).

MANNINGHAM, JOHN—Diary of John Manningham 1602-3, edited John Bruce (Camden Society).

NEWCOME, HENRY—The Diary of the Rev. Henry Newcome 1661-1663, edited T. Heywood (Chetham Society).

NORTH, ROGER—The Autobiography of the Hon. Roger North, contained in Vol. III of Lives of the Norths, edited A. Jessopp.

NORTHBROOKE, JOHN—A Treatise against Dicing, Dancing, Plays, and Interludes with other idle pastimes, 1577, edition of 1843.

ORDINANCES—Acts and Ordinances of the Interregnum 1642-1660, edited C. H. Firth and R. S. Rait.

PEPYS, SAMUEL—Diary of Samuel Pepys, deciphered by J. Smith, notes by Richard Lord Braybrooke (Everyman Edition).

PRESBYTERIAN—The Presbyterian Movement in the reign of Queen Elizabeth, as illustrated by the Minute Book of the Dedham Classis 1582-1589, edited R. G. Usher (Camden Society).

PROCLAMATIONS—Tudor and Stuart Proclamations, calendared by R. Steele.

PRYNNE, WILLIAM—Canterburies Doome, edition of 1646.
—A Divine Tragedy, edition of MDCXXXVI.

—Histriomastix, The Players Scourge, edition 1633.

RAWDON, MARMADUKE—The Life of Marmaduke Rawdon of York, edited R. Davies (Camden Society).

ROGERS, THOMAS—The Catholic Doctrine of the Church of England, edition of 1607, edited by J. J. S. Perowne (Parker Society).

RUSHWORTH, JOHN—Historical Collections 1629-1640, edition of 1680.

SABBATH—Treatise on the Sabbath, Primerose 1636: under this heading are bound together in the edition in Dr. Williams's Library.

    1. A Treatise of the Sabbath by David Primerose, 1636.

    2. The Doctrine of the Sabbath by Dr. Prideaux, edition of 1634.

    3. A Sovereign Antidote Against Sabbatarian Errors, edition of 1636.

    4. An Examination and Confutation of a Lawless Pamphlet by Dr. F. White, 1637.

    5. A Sabbath of Rest to be kept by the Saints, by Nicholas Smith, 1675.

    6. A Vindication of Certain Passages in a Sermon of the morality of the Sabbath by Giles Collier, 1653.

    7. A Learned Treatise of the Sabbath, by Edward Brerewood, 1631.

SALISBURY—Calendar of Manuscripts of the Marquis of Salisbury.

SANDERSON, ROBERT—Works, collected by W. Jacobson, edition of MDCCCLIV, Vol. V.

SECONDE PARTE OF A REGISTER—MSS. in Dr. Williams's Library: The Seconde Parte of a Register, edited A. Peel.

STETTIN—Diary of the Journey of Philip Julius, Duke of Stettin-Pomerania, through England 1602, edited by Von Bülow (Transactions of the Royal Historical Society 1892).

STATUTES—Statutes at Large, edition of MDCCCXI.

STUBBES, PHILIP—Anatomy of the Abuses in England in Shakespeare's Youth, 1583, edited F. J. Furnivall.

SYMONDS, RICHARD—Diary of the Marches of the Royal Army During the Great Civil War, edited C. E. Long (Camden Society).

THORNTON, ALICE—Autobiography of Mrs. Alice Thornton, edited C. Jackson (Surtees Society).

TREVELYAN—Trevelyan Papers, Part III, edited W. C. and C. E. Trevelyan (Camden Society).

TWISSE, WILLIAM—Of the Morality of the Fourth Commandment, 1641.

VAUX, LAURENCE—A Catechisme or Christian Doctrine, 1583, edited T. G. Law (Chetham Society).

WALSINGHAM, FRANCIS—Journal of Sir Francis Walsingham 1570-1583, edited C. T. Martin (Camden Society).

WILKINS—Concilia Magnœ Britanniœ et Hiberniœ edition of MDCCXXXVII, Vol. IV.

YONGE, WALTER—Diary of Walter Yonge 1604-1628, edited G. Roberts (Camden Society).

B.   Books containing extracts from County and Town Records of the sixteenth and seventeenth centuries.

DEVON—Quarter Sessions from Queen Elizabeth to Queen Anne, by A. H. A. Hamilton.

EXETER—Gleanings from the Municipal and Cathedral Records of the City of Exeter, by W. Cotton and H. Woollcombe.

HERTFORD—County Records, Notes and Extracts from the Sessions Rolls 1581-1698, edited W. J. Hardy.

LANCASHIRE—Quarter Sessions Records, Vol. I, edited J. Tait (Chetham Society).

MANCHESTER—Sessions, Vol. I, 1616-1623, edited E. Axon, (Record Society).

MIDDLESEX—County Records, Vols. II and III, edited J. C. Jeaffreson.

SOMERSET—Quarter Session Records, Vol. III, edited E. H. Bates Harbin.

WORCESTER—County Records, Quarter Sessions, Papers 1591-1643, edited J. W. W. Bund.

YORKSHIRE—Quarter Sessions Records of the North Riding of the County of York, edited J. C. Atkinson.

C.   Books written since the end of the seventeenth century.

BESANT, WALTER—London in the Time of the Tudors (1904).

—London in the Time of the Stuarts (1903).

BRAND, JOHN—Popular Antiquities of Great Britain, edited by W. C. Hazlitt (1870).

CARTER, T. T.—Nicholas Ferrar, his household and his friends (1892).

COLLIER, JEREMY—An Ecclesiastical History of Great Britain, Vol. II (1714).

COLLIER, J. PAYNE—The History of English Dramatic Poetry to the time of Shakespeare and Annals of the Stage to the Restoration (1879).

COX, ROBERT—Sabbath Laws and Sabbath Duties (1853).
—Literature of the Sabbath Question (1865).

DAVIS, H. W. C.—Mediaeval England, a new edition of Barnard's Companion to English History (1924).

DISRAELI, ISAAC—Character of James I, from Vol. VI of Works of Disraeli, edited B. Disraeli (1869).

FRERE, W. H.—The English Church in the reign of Elizabeth and James I (1904).

GARDINER, S. R.—History of England, 1603-1642 (1883).

GEE, HENRY—Documents Illustrative of English Church History by H. Gee and W. J. Hardy (1896).
—The Elizabeth Clergy and the Settlement of Religion 1558-1564 (1898).

GIBSON, EDMUND—Codex Juris Ecclesiastici Anglicano, Vol. I (1761).

GOVETT, L. A.—The King's Book of Sports (1890).

GRIFFITH, W.—The Sabbath (19th century publication, no date).

HENSON, H. HENSLEY—Studies in English Religion in the Seventeenth Century (1903).

HESSEY, JAMES AUGUSTUS—Sunday, Its Origin, History and present obligation (Bampton Lecture for 1860).

LEWIS, A. H.—A Critical History of Sunday Legislation (1888).

NEAL, DANIEL—The History of the Puritans (1822).

NEALE, EDWARD VANSITTART—Feasts and Fasts (1845).

NICHOLS, JOHN—The Progresses of King James I (1828).

NOTES AND QUERIES, 2nd Series, Vol. VIII.

SHAW, W. A.—Article in Victoria County History of Lancashire, Vol. II.

STRUTT, JOSEPH—The Sports and Pastimes of the People of England, new edition, edited by J. C. Cox (1903).

STRYPE, JOHN—Annals of the Reformation (1824).
—Life and Acts of John Aylmer (1821).
—Life and Acts of John Whitgift (1822).
—Ecclesiastical Memorials (1822).
—Life of Grindal (1821).
—Life and Acts of Matthew Parker (1821).
TREVELYAN, G. M.—England Under the Stuarts (1910).
—History of England (1926).
TREVELYAN, W. B.—Sunday (1902).
TRAILL, H. D.—Social England, edited H. D. Traill and
    J. S. Mann, Vol. IV.
TROTTER, ELEANOR—Seventeenth Century Life in the
    Country Parish (1919).
WARE, S. L.—The Elizabethan Parish in its Ecclesiastical
    and Financial Aspects (1908).
WEBB, SIDNEY AND BEATRICE—The History of Liquor
    Licensing in England (1903).

INDEX

Vestments, 21
Victualling-house, 147, 150, 193
Vincent, 159
Vintners, 118

W

Waggoner, 45, 113, 114, 158, 162, 192
Wakes—see under Ales and Feasts
Walsingham, Sir F., 30
Warwick, Sir P., 204
Washing, 162
Weaver (silk), 195
Webb, S. and B., 172
West, 159
Westminster Assembly, 170
Whalley, Major-General, 159
Whitsuntide, 156
Wilkins's Concilia, 25, 28, 51

Wiltshire, 175
Worcestershire, 81, 82, 101, 102, 119, 139
Work on Sunday, 13-17, 19, 20, 22, 25, 26, 29, 30, 32, 37, 49, 51, 58, 59, 65, 66, 71, 72, 73, 79, 80, 81, 97, 105, 113, 115, 117, 118, 119, 133, 135, 140, 141, 145, 146, 147, 149, 152, 154, 155, 157, 158, 161, 162, 163, 164, 165, 170, 174, 181, 183, 184, 186, 187, 192, 193, 195, 196, 202, 203, 204, 206, 207
Wrestling, 149, 155, 162, 197

Y

Yorkshire, 73, 74, 75, 101, 175, 177, 196
Yonge, W., 77, 109

Made and Printed in Great Britain by Ebenezer Baylis & Son, Ltd., The Trinity Press, Worcester, and London.